What's That
BIRD?

Worth Watching
Colorful, alert, resourceful, and endowed with the gift of flight, birds — like this Rose-breasted Grosbeak — have fascinated people for centuries.

What's That
BIRD?

Getting to Know the Birds Around You,
Coast-to-Coast

Joseph Choiniere & Claire Mowbray Golding

Photography by Tom Vezo • Illustrations by James Robins

Storey Publishing

The mission of Storey Publishing is to serve our customers
by publishing practical information that encourages personal independence
in harmony with the environment.

Edited by Deborah Burns and Sarah Guare
Art direction and design by Wendy Palitz
Text production by Vicky Vaughn and Jennifer Jepson Smith
Cover and Interior Photographs by © Tom Vezo, except for the following: Courtesy of Bushnell
  Performance Optics 41; J. S. Lang/VIREO 15; Courtesy of the Lear/Carson Collection,
  Connecticut College/Photo by Harris & Ewing 92 left; Library of Congress, Prints and
  Photographs Division (LC-DIG-ppmsca-02905DLC) 92 right; ©Anthony Mercieca vii, 11
  inset, 13 top, 36, 49 right, 52 left, 57 right, 60 right, 66 right, 104 bottom, 105 top left, 106
  bottom, 109 middle, 110 bottom; © A. L. Perry 108 top; © Photodisk/Getty Images front
  cover bottom; Used with permission of the Division of Birds, Smithsonian Institution,
  Washington DC 79; © D. Tipling/VIREO 106 top; © Doug Wechsler/VIREO 107 bottom.

Illustrations by © James Robins

Bird Silhouettes and Range Maps by Ilona Sherratt

Indexed by Jan Williams

Storey books are available for special premium and promotional uses and for customized edi-
tions. For further information, please call 1-800-793-9396.

Printed in China by Elegance Printing
10 9 8 7 6 5 4 3 2 1

Library of Congress Cataloging-in-Publication Data

Choiniere, Joseph.
  What's that bird? : getting to know the birds around you, coast-to-coast / Joseph Choiniere
and Claire Mowbray Golding.
      p. cm.
  Includes bibliographical references and index.
  ISBN 1-58017-554-6 (pb : alk. paper) — ISBN 1-58017-555-4 (hc w/jacket : alk. paper)
  1. Birds—Juvenile literature. 2. Bird watching—Juvenile literature. I. Golding, Claire
Mowbray. II. Title.

QL676.2.C4875 2005
598—dc22
                              2004017307

Dedication

For Jeanne, who started my bird adventures, and Helen, who wouldn't let me stop. — JC

For my parents, who had to keep the birds away, and also for Donc, Heather, and Emma, who first made me want to bring them closer. — CMG

Mourning Dove

Acknowledgments

No book is the sole creation of its authors. For their painstaking reading of the manuscript and invaluable advice, we thank Dr. Ed Armstrong, Chris Eaton, and Carl and Elizabeth Sladek. Jen Hilt, Helen Bartucca, and Hanna Geshelin reviewed parts of the manuscript in its early stages and offered consistent encouragement, as did The Mountain Writers Guild of Princeton. We're also indebted to The New England newsletter of the Society of Children's Book Writers and Illustrators, an outstanding small publication that first alerted us to Storey's request for proposals. We thank Barry W. VanDusen for sharing his beautiful birding journals with us, and Joann Blum for very kindly searching for an elusive photograph. Without Deborah Burns, Sarah Guare, and the dedicated and careful staff at Storey Publishing, this book would be very different; they've worked just as hard as we have — maybe harder! — to make it both attractive and useful. And of course we save our sweetest songs for our long-suffering families, who often wondered where we'd gone, and why we bothered each other with phone calls and emails on holidays, birthdays, and anniversaries over the past two-and-a-half years. To all of you, a big thank you! Enjoy!

Gotcha!
A Great Crested Flycatcher pauses to savor a quick bite, probably caught on the wing.

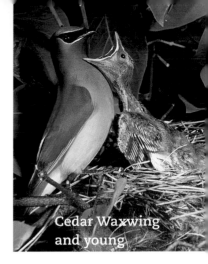

Cedar Waxwing
and young

Contents

What a show!
This Blue Jay's feathers are a visual feast of color, texture, and pattern. How many different blues can you spot in just this one bird?

1

Meet the Bird

Being introduced to a bird might seem a bit silly. After all, if you step outside your door, birds are right there waiting for you, whether you live in Manhattan or Millers Falls. But do you *really* know birds? Can you tell a flank from a rump, an eyeline from an eye ring? Do you know how much your arm is like a bird's wing? If not, read on!

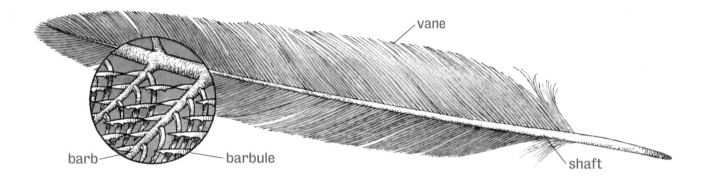

vane

barb — barbule

shaft

A feather may look smooth to your naked eye, but use a magnifying glass and you'll see how complex its structure really is.

Feather facts

The first thing you should know about birds is that they're the only creatures on earth with feathers. A **feather** is a body outgrowth, a scale that has evolved over time to keep birds warm and dry and to help with flight. Individual feathers are made up of a central **shaft** with a broad and flexible **vane**. The vane is made up of hundreds of tiny parallel branches, called **barbs**. The barbs, in turn, have their own branches, called **barbules**, covered with little hooks that interlock with other barbules in a "web" that creates the feather vane. That's not, however, the end of the story.

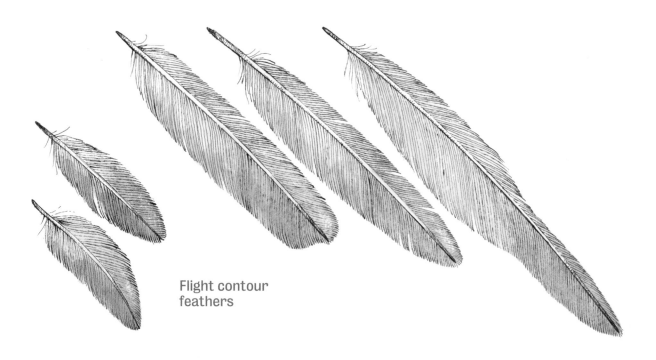

Flight contour feathers

Feather types

All feathers on a bird are not the same. In fact, there are several types of feathers, and each type serves a different purpose.

Contour feathers form the basic outer shape of the bird, including wings, tail, and body. Flight contour feathers, including wings and tail, are longer and have stiff shafts. Body contour feathers are shorter and have softer parts near the base of the shaft to help with insulation: keeping the bird warm in cold weather and cool in warm weather. Contour feathers protect the bird's body and help it fly.

Q. True Pigment, or Reflected Light?

A. If you find a blue or green feather (Blue Jay feathers are some of the most common finds), hold it up and look through it. The blue color will disappear and seem black or brown. That's because the light is no longer reflected to your eye. Next, try a yellow or red feather (look near your bird feeder for American Goldfinch or Northern Cardinal feathers). No matter how you hold it, the color will remain visible. The color is actually a part of these feathers, not just reflected from them.

Northern Cardinal

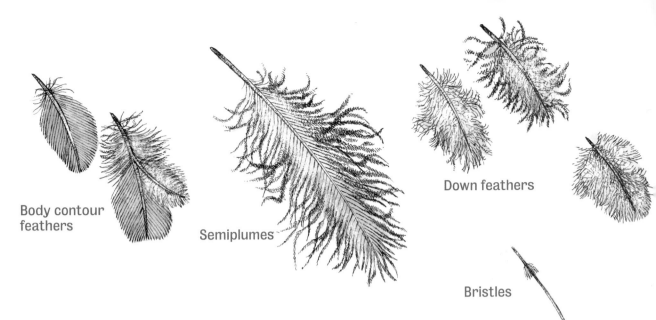

Body contour feathers

Semiplumes

Down feathers

Bristles

If you have ever found a large feather on a walk outdoors, it's probably a wing or tail feather. A wing feather will be asymmetrical (not the same shape on both sides of the shaft), which provides aerodynamic lift.

Semiplumes fill the space between contour feathers and the next layer of feathers, called down. Semiplumes have large shafts with downy barbs.

Down feathers are hidden under the contour feathers on adult birds. Young birds often have their down showing, as their contour feathers have not grown in yet. Down feathers are entirely soft and insulate the bird against extreme temperatures. If you have a down vest or comforter, you'll know how it feels to be an eider duck or a goose!

Bristles are feathers that look more like hairs. They are found mostly around the eyes, nostrils, and mouths of birds. Some even extend right through the contour feathers. Bristles give birds the sense of touch, much the same way as whiskers do for mammals.

Unruffling Your Feathers

Find a bird's feather, and look for the barbules under a magnifying glass. If you split the feather's barbs apart, you can magically reconnect them using a pencil as your "beak" and gently stroking the feather from shaft to outside of vane.

Feather colors can be spectacular. The colors are formed either by pigments (natural coloring) or by the structure of the feather itself. Reds and yellows are usually true pigments. Blues and greens are created by prismlike feather barbs and the way they reflect or refract light. And what about those birds that seem to be a different color from every angle? Their feathers are **iridescent,** meaning the feathers' structure causes them to reflect many gradations of color and seem to shimmer.

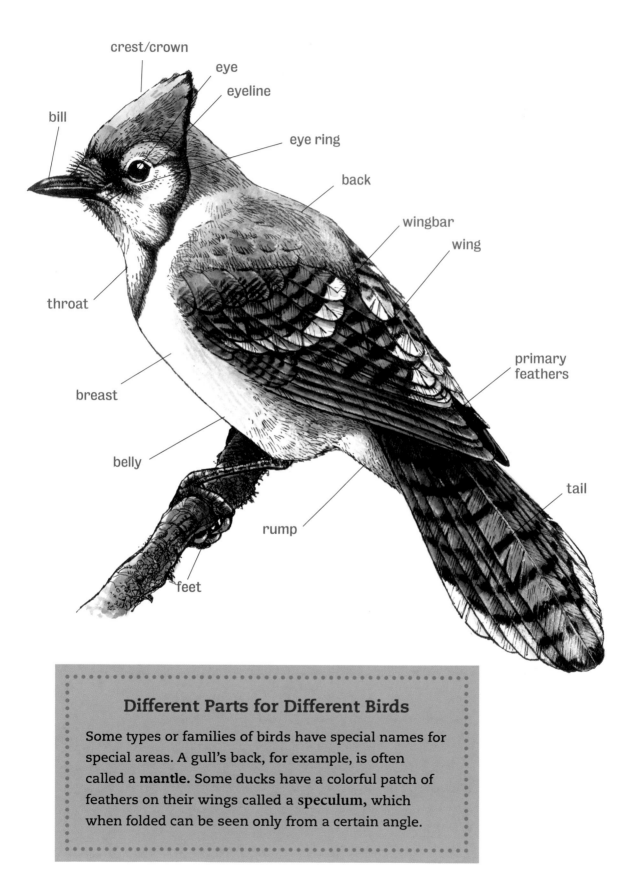

crest/crown

eye

eyeline

bill

eye ring

back

wingbar

wing

throat

primary
feathers

breast

belly

tail

rump

feet

Different Parts for Different Birds

Some types or families of birds have special names for
special areas. A gull's back, for example, is often
called a **mantle.** Some ducks have a colorful patch of
feathers on their wings called a **speculum,** which
when folded can be seen only from a certain angle.

flank

primary
feathers

undertail

breast

rump

wingbar

Bird Anatomy 101

A bird's **topography,** shown here, is like a map that tells you the
names of various areas of the bird. It's good to know the names of
these areas because other bird-watchers and field guides use them
to help identify birds.

Some areas are really structures, like feet. They're described on
page 6 of this chapter. Some parts, like the head, have many small
details worth knowing *(eye ring, eyeline, crest);* other parts have
few. Many areas also have two names, a scientific name and a
common-use name, like *superciliary* and *eyebrow.*

The structures of birds

Feathers make any bird a bird. But birds' feet, wings, and bills take very different forms in different birds. These structures can help tell you what a bird eats, how it flies, and where it might be able to land.

Multipurpose feet

Birds have very unusual, flexible, and highly developed feet. Like human feet, which allow us to balance ourselves and walk, birds' feet are made the way they are for many purposes.

When you take a walk, you probably walk on your whole foot, from heel to toes. Most birds walk only on their toes. And while other flying animals, like bats or butterflies, walk on four or six legs, birds walk on just two. Whether you're watching a flightless Ostrich or a speedy Peregrine Falcon, only two feet carry it around when it's on the ground.

Scales form a protective covering over most birds' feet and toes. Scales appear in many different sizes and arrangements. Thrushes look like they're wearing boots, since one long scale covers the lower foot bone. Some shorebirds have very small and irregular scales that form patterns like mosaic tiles. Scales can be temporary, too. The Ruffed Grouse grows "snowshoes" every winter: Scaly fringes along the sides of its toes help it stay on top of the snow. The fringes disappear in summer, when they're not needed.

Have you ever wondered how birds manage to hold on to pencil-thin branches or land gracefully in water? **Claws** help birds dig into uneven surfaces and grasp small objects. **Webbing,** a thin, flexible skin between the bones of the feet, allows waterbirds to swim both on and below the water's surface. Webbing helps with walking, too. The Wood Duck may walk her ducklings more than half a mile to water, after they hatch in a hollow tree.

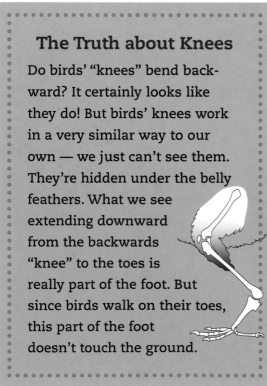

The Truth about Knees

Do birds' "knees" bend backward? It certainly looks like they do! But birds' knees work in a very similar way to our own — we just can't see them. They're hidden under the belly feathers. What we see extending downward from the backwards "knee" to the toes is really part of the foot. But since birds walk on their toes, this part of the foot doesn't touch the ground.

Feet Feats

The three birds shown here have very different feet, all well suited to the way they live. Hooked claws called **talons** allow the American Kestrel (*top*) to grip high perches, and to catch and hold the grasshoppers and mice it feeds on. Watch a Mallard (*middle*) land sometime, and you'll see how well this duck's webbed feet work as landing gear. Extra large feet on a tiny White-breasted Nuthatch (*bottom*) give it the ability to hang upside down and move easily on rough bark as it searches for insect eggs.

Wings

Which animals have wings? Not just birds, but birds have certainly developed wings to a greater extent than any other animal. Bats are the only other **vertebrates** (animals with backbones) that truly fly.

Most of a bird's inner and outer structure is designed for flight. Here's all you'd need if you wanted to fly, too:

- A streamlined, tapering shape
- Huge flight muscles (the breast meat of your chicken or turkey dinner)
- A lightweight skull without heavy teeth
- A useable tail made mostly of feathers (no bones or muscles to drag you down!)
- The ability to change your direction in a split second at 50 miles an hour

The bird's larger flight feathers are called primaries and secondaries, and they form the wing surface. Arm, hand, and finger bones have grown together and been adapted to support flight.

All birds have **primaries,** flight feathers attached to a modified wrist and hand. Only three digits, the thumb and first two fingers, remain. Most of the bird's outer wing feathers (the primaries) attach to their second and third digits and to their combined wrist–hand bone, called the **carpo-metacarpus.**

The other part of the bird's long flight feathers, closer to the body, are called **secondaries.** These feathers are attached to a forearm bone, the **ulna.** The upper arm bone, the **humerus,** is quite large and helps power flight energy from the sternum and chest muscles out to the wing. The bird's thumb is movable and tiny and connects to a couple of small stiff feathers on the top of the wing, called the **alula.** These feathers, when moved, change the way air flows over the wing, aiding flight.

Flying mechanics

In order to fly, and especially in order to soar, birds must be able to control and balance the forces of lift, their own weight, and

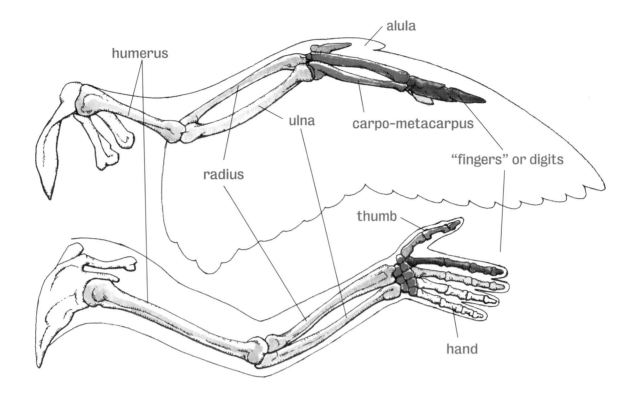

humerus

alula

ulna

carpo-metacarpus

radius

"fingers" or digits

thumb

hand

A wing *(top)* and an arm have a similar structure.

their speed. High in the air, the wind can change quickly from gusts to calm, and birds must change their flight speeds often in response. A solid wing doesn't offer the fine control they need to handle these forces, so soaring birds have **slots**. Slots are spaces created between the primary feathers on the wing tips. Air forced upward through the slot expands again, reducing pressure above the wing and giving lift. Slots also direct the air flowing over and under the wings and balance it.

Feather Slots

Can you recognize a Turkey Vulture? These big birds with huge wingspans can often be seen, alone or in groups, hovering high above a field. But have you ever seen them flap those big wings? Probably not. They balance in the air by tilting their wings and using slots to stay aloft.

A Tale of Tails

Birds actually lack tails. True tails, like those of a squirrel or a cat, have a bony internal structure and are covered with flesh, as well as hair or scales. Birds look as if they have tails somewhat like these, but their tails are actually made only from sturdy feathers and a tiny bit of bone or flesh.

Wing shapes

The shape of a bird's wings can help tell you which bird you're looking at and how it flies. Ornithologists group wing shapes according to the wing's length, width, shape of tip, and how the wing curves underneath, from cupped to flat. Ruffed Grouse have short, broad wings, rounded at the tip and cupped underneath, so they can take off quickly and maneuver in dense woods. Terns, on the other hand, have long, narrow, pointed wings, flat underneath, that let them fly fast for a long time and change direction like acrobats in midair.

Wings don't do all the work of flying, however. Tail feathers are flight feathers, too: Birds couldn't fly without them. A bird's tail functions as a rudder in flight and as a brake when the bird wants to slow down or stop.

The Ruffed Grouse (*inset*) has blunt-looking wings that are shorter than its body. This grouse is "drumming": vibrating his wings very rapidly to produce a whirring, drumlike sound that attracts females. The Common Tern, on the other hand, has narrow, pointed wings that are longer than its body, giving it speed and allowing it to perform miraculous in-air maneuvers.

Hitting the Wall

When birds hit windows or cars, sometimes their chest muscles are bruised, making it very painful to breathe. They need rest in a dark, quiet place and, often, medication to relax their systems.

How birds breathe

The way birds breathe is very different from the way other vertebrates, like humans, breathe. Birds need lots of oxygen to supply their flight muscles, but they have very small lungs and no diaphragm. Instead, they have an extensive system of air sacs in their chest and abdomen. This system allows the bird to breathe continuously, with each breathing cycle requiring two breaths in (inhalation) and two breaths out (exhalation).

Here's how it works: When a bird breathes in, the incoming air goes right through a part of the lung and into the abdominal

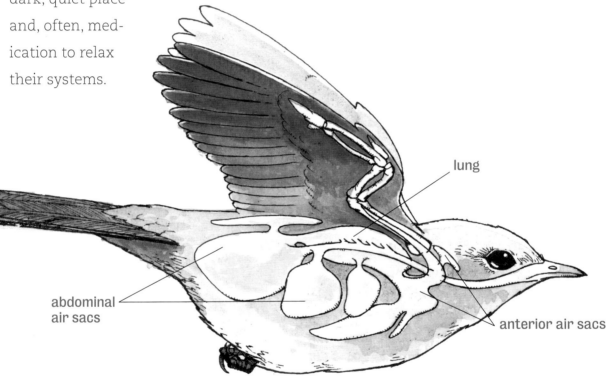

lung

abdominal air sacs

anterior air sacs

Q. What Are Wishbones Really For?

A. A bird's wishbone has another purpose besides wishes: It acts as a spring. When the bird's wings flap downward, the wishbone opens and stores some energy. It snaps back to help push the wings upward again. The wishbone's movements are timed to open and close the air sacs, too, and help the bird breathe as it flies.

Did You Know?
Different birds breathe at different rates. Hummingbirds at rest breathe about 143 times a minute; turkeys only about 7 times a minute.

air sacs, inflating them. When the bird breathes out, these air sacs fill up another part of the lung, where blood picks up oxygen from the air. The second time the bird inhales, air in the lungs is driven out and fills anterior air sacs in the upper chest. When the bird exhales the second time, the stale air leaves its body. So, in a way, the bird's lungs get air when it breathes *out!* And birds exchange almost all the air in their lungs with every breath, which keeps them well supplied with oxygen at all times.

Bill types

Remember when people were always telling you to chew your food properly? You'd never hear that if you were a bird. Birds *can't* chew their food, as they don't have true teeth. Instead, they rip their food into small pieces, crush berries, break up vegetation, and then swallow it whole. They use their **bills** (also called beaks) instead of teeth to help capture, hold, and chop food apart. Some birds even use their bills to strain food from water.

 **ducks:** flat, wide, spoonlike bill for scooping and straining

 **warblers:** narrow, pointy, insect-grabbing bill, like tweezers

 **woodpeckers:** sharp, strong, solid bill for punching holes in hard wood

 **thrashers:** curved bill for pushing leaves aside in search of insects

Bills are bony outgrowths of the bird's skull. Several bones are fused together to form the upper and lower parts of the bill, called **mandibles.** The bill is covered by a horny sheath made of keratin, the same protein that forms your fingernails and birds' claws, feathers, and scales.

Birds' bills give you important clues about what they eat and can also help you with identification. Below are a few common groups of birds and the food for which their bills are best suited.

sparrows: triangular, cone-like bill for breaking and crushing

The Incredible, Flexible Bill

American Woodcocks have five-inch bills that they use to reach deep into leaf litter and soil in their forest habitats. There they grab earthworms and other invertebrates for food. Their bills can both sense their prey underground *and* flex at the tip, like tweezers, to grab a worm or grub underground, so they don't need to dig.

flycatchers: pointed bill with a downward hook to help grab and hold insects in midair

hawks: curved, heavy bill for tearing and prying flesh; notched to hold prey

The remarkable raven

Birds have many notable characteristics, but some species stand out for their exceptional abilities. Meet the Common Raven, a remarkable bird, and the largest North American songbird. He's a great example of how well equipped birds are to meet the demands of their everyday lives. Compare his senses to yours. Can you match his abilities?

Brain

- Ravens learn to count more quickly than monkeys do.

- Here's processing speed that puts computers to shame: Ravens maneuver easily around objects while flying at 30 miles per hour. They can fly wing-to-wing and head-to-head with a mate when courting.

- Ravens think ahead: They pile their meat, biting off chunks and stacking them, then gobble the whole pile into their mouth-pouch and carry it off.

- Ravens love to play, which is a sign of intelligence. Ravens clown around by hanging from their beaks, hanging upside down by only one foot, or rolling on their backs. And each raven plays differently, which shows that this is not innate behavior.

Sight

- Ravens' eyes are large, making up as much as 15 percent of the weight of their skulls.

- Ravens' eyesight is excellent; they can see prey on the ground from a half mile in the air!

- Ravens can focus quickly, which enables them to absorb all the information from a scene in a mere glance.

Smell

- Although their other senses are impressive, ravens aren't known to have a great sense of smell.

Hearing

- Ravens, like most birds, have well-developed hearing, which helps them escape predators and find prey.

- Ravens can hear and mimic a specific human voice.

Voice

- Ravens can talk as well as or better than parrots.

- Ravens have a large repertoire of calls that make up their own little raven language.

- Ravens have some musical ability; rather than using song, they use calls, yells, and other sounds.

2

How Birds Live

To a casual observer, birds' lives may seem simple: They eat, fly, chirp, nest, and raise their young. If that's all you want to know about birds, you can still be a contented bird watcher. But if you're the kind of person who wonders why those little gray birds like the bark of that tree, or where that huge bird is headed when it flies over the swamp every morning, you'll find there's plenty to know about bird life. It might even be more complicated than your own!

Where's home?

At first glance, birds seem to live everywhere: from north to south, hot to cold, in dry deserts, soggy rainforests, city, country, suburb, and your own backyard. And so many kinds of birds **migrate** — move from place to place according to the seasons — that explaining where birds live can be complicated. If you asked a Palm Warbler where he lives, he might say something like this:

"I live in a Western Hemisphere northern forest in open bogs larger than three acres with wooded margins of stunted spruce or tamarack, at the base of small shrubs, in mossy groundcover. But that's just in summer."

Are you sorry you asked? Let's try again.

For these two Red-tailed Hawk nestlings, home is a mass of sticks in a saguaro cactus in the desert of Arizona.

There's no place like habitat

Where do *you* live? Near the ocean? In a big city on flat plains? Wherever you live, there are certain types of trees, plants, bodies of water, rocks, soil, animals, and insects that form the world around you. This is your **habitat,** your natural environment. Everything in the environment, living and nonliving, is part of your habitat.

Birds have habitats, too. About 9,500 **species,** or kinds, of birds can be found on our planet, and they inhabit every nook and cranny of every continent. Yet most individual bird species are very picky about where they'll live.

Remember the American Woodcock with its flexible bill, from page 15? That bill enables the woodcock to dig deep to find worms and insects in its young forest habitat. But if it lived in the Arctic tundra, the woodcock's bill would knock against the permafrost and be useless. Birds prefer to live in the habitats where they fit best.

Changing Scene
A beautiful red maple swamp, home to Gray Catbirds, Yellow Warblers, and Virginia Rail, will change when beavers move in.

Pine trees

Red maple trees

Gray Catbird

Yellow Warbler

Virginia Rail

Birds fit well in certain habitats because they have **adapted,** or changed over many years, to function well in them. Their preferred habitats give them the food, shelter, nest materials, and climate they need to survive and thrive.

Never a dull moment

You might think of your community or neighborhood as pretty much the same as it's always been. But a bird's habitat is always changing. It changes with the seasons, of course. It also changes year by year.

Unfortunately, natural habitats are quickly being replaced with non-natural materials in many parts of North America. If too many grassy fields become asphalt parking lots, for example, some bird species may not survive. That's why most efforts to save birds focus on saving their habitats.

New Opportunities
When beavers flood the swamp, the rail, catbirds, and warblers move off. Other species move in.

Mallards

Great Blue Heron nest

Dead pine trees

Green Heron

Beaver lodge

Wood Duck

Why that habitat?

Why do certain birds prefer certain habitats? There are lots of places birds could live within any habitat. But each bird species has its own "wish list" of conditions.

Black-throated Blue Warblers, for example, nest in northeastern North America in forests. Their forest habitat has to be a certain size, however: Twenty pairs of Black-throated Blue Warblers can live in 1,000 acres of forest, but 100 acres can be too small for two pairs to live in. They seem to need fairly large blocks of forest. For nesting, they also prefer a dense layer of vegetation in the **shrub layer,** the forest's tangle of branches and leaves that reaches from the ground to about 10 feet above the ground. That's why forests containing dense, impenetrable thickets of mountain laurel are especially popular with these warblers.

Winter homes, summer homes

Do you know families who spend summers in one home and the rest of the year in another? Many birds have more than one home during the year. Chickadees, for example, migrate locally. The Black-capped Chickadees that come to your feeder in winter may spend the summer in forests not far away, nesting in small holes in trees, then return in groups to spend winter close to your house.

Some North American waterbirds, such as the Common Eider, nest in the tundra, then spend winter in floating "rafts," or groups, of eiders in the open sea farther south.

Forest layers
Each of these birds (*opposite*) has different needs, so each makes use of a different layer of this forest habitat. The male Black-throated Blue Warbler gleans caterpillars from the high leaves of the canopy. The Eastern Wood-Pewee "hawks" flying insects in open spaces in the mid-canopy. The Gray Catbird feeds on heavily-laden fruiting shrubs lower down. The Eastern Towhee thrashes out beetles in dense grasses and dead leaves.

Q. What Is a Forest?

A. Forests are habitats made up mostly of trees. Trees provide shade, which keeps the soil moister and the temperatures cooler beneath them. Trees are also tall, and many layers of vegetation develop beneath them. In these layers, the shade and moisture vary, making them welcome habitats for different bird species.

Try this: Stand at the edge of a forest or a small stand of trees for half an hour. Where do you see birds? Are they in the top, middle, or lower part of the trees?

Black-throated
Blue Warbler

canopy

Eastern Wood-Pewee

mid-canopy

Gray Catbird

Eastern
Towhee

shrub layer

herb layer

The Winter Menu

Winter foods for birds can be plentiful, but foods are often spread far apart. For example, the white ash tree produces lots of seeds, but the trees themselves are scattered over a large area of forest. To make the work of food-finding easier, some birds work in feeding flocks made up of different bird species. They spread out and find food, then alert the rest of the flock. In the Northeast, Black-capped Chickadees, Tufted Titmice, White-breasted Nuthatches, and Brown Creepers can often be seen together in flocks.

A bird's diet

Do the beef or beans, bananas or potato chips you eat grow outside your window? Probably not! In our culture, food often comes to us by truck or airplane, and not very many of us choose our home according to what foods are available there. It's different for birds. They choose their habitat mostly because of the food it offers. Several species of bird can share the same habitat, but they generally don't eat the same foods, so they don't compete with each other.

Birds eat almost anything and everything from the plant and animal kingdoms, including other birds and other birds' eggs. From tiny algae or bacteria to mammals the size of a fox, from lowly water mosses to the high buds of enormous poplar trees — all these, and more, can be part of their diet. Birds also eat human crops, like corn, rice, and wheat, as well as acorns and tree sap.

Some birds, like robins and crows, aren't fussy about their diets. They're known as **generalists:** They'll eat fruit, meat, insects, seeds — whatever's around. **Specialists,** on the other hand, have one main food source. For hummingbirds it's nectar, although they'll catch insects from time to time to get the nitrogen they need. Owls and hawks are strictly meat-eaters; crossbills specialize in the seeds of evergreen cones.

When do birds eat?

Birds eat during most of the time they are active, and they are active at different times, depending on their species. **Diurnal** birds are active in daylight; **nocturnal** birds at night; **crepuscular** birds at dawn and dusk. You might find a variety of birds feeding in the same place at different times of day. American Robins, Common Flickers, American Woodcocks, and Whip-poor-wills, for example, might all use the same lawn and forest edge and capture worms and insects. But because they feed at different times, in different ways, and on different worms and insects, they peacefully share the space.

Did You Know?
Birds eat often and a lot. Tiny birds, like wrens, eat much more for their body weight than do larger birds, like hawks. Birds eat anywhere from 5 to 100 percent of their body weight daily.

Q. Do Birds Drink Water?

A. Yes, they do! Although they don't sweat, as people do, they can lose lots of water through respiration, or breathing. So they need to drink when they can. They also get some water from their food.

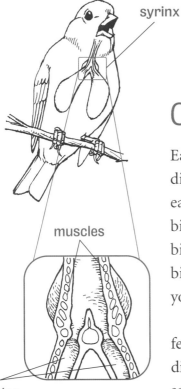
syrinx

muscles

windpipe

Controlled by muscles, the syrinx allows birds to create amazing sounds.

Conversing and communicating

Each species of bird has a distinct song: That is, the songs are distinct to the birds themselves. You may not always find them easy to tell apart! But songs can be very useful to you in your bird-watching adventures. Songs can help you find birds, identify birds that don't show themselves, and tell you something about a bird's behavior. A song might even give away where a nest is, if you can learn the language! Songs are, above all, beautiful.

Although males do most of the singing, both males and females call or sound alarm notes. Here's a quick bird language dictionary: A bird's **song** is a short or long series of notes that often sound musical. Usually heard in spring and early summer, it is used to define territory (see page 28) and attract and communicate with a mate. A **call** is a single note or series of notes that isn't musical, and an **alarm note** is a short, urgent call.

Q. Do Female Birds Sing?

A. Some do. The Northern Cardinal is one: She learns her mate's song by singing it back to him, and eventually they sing it together. Some ornithologists think that this allows her to find her mate. That may not seem like such a difficult task, until you realize that a cardinal's territory is the size of a small backyard, and its song is quite loud. Imagine a neighborhood full of calling cardinals: It would be helpful to know which one was calling for you!

Birds sing for many reasons: to tell other birds they are there, to attract mates, to communicate with their own species and other species. Songs are part of a bird's language.

Ever tried to imitate a bird by singing or whistling? Pretty tough, isn't it? Birds, the most musical of all animals, don't create their songs in the same way you do. Instead, many have a unique structure in their windpipe called the **syrinx,** which looks a little like an elephant's head with two trunks (in miniature, of course, since it fits inside their throats!). The syrinx is controlled by muscles: It can stretch or enlarge and change its diameter. That's what makes birds masters of creating and controlling sound. Some birds, like the Veery, can even sing two songs at once — one in each half of the syrinx!

Most birds have a repertoire of call notes, alarm notes, and songs. But those aren't their only forms of communication. Some, like the Mourning Dove, also use their wings to create sounds. Others, like the Downy Woodpecker, drum with their beaks on hollow trees to attract females.

No Room! No Room!

Mimicry, the art of sounding like someone other than yourself, is a particular talent of some birds. The Gray Catbird, for example, imitates so many birds that it often convinces outsiders that its territory is full. The catbird then conveniently has more space (and food) for itself!

You're Invading my Space!
This bird is in your face, pumping its chest, flashing the red feather insignia "epaulets" on its shoulders. It's telling you that you are in its territory. It's a male Red-winged Blackbird, using bird vocal and body language to claim its place in a wetland, where it nests with many others of the same species. Birds often combine displays of feather shape and color with other actions to make their territorial points.

Communities of birds

In your community, your neighbors might be a few feet or a few miles away. Like humans, birds may live close to each other or much farther apart. Also like humans, birds form family groups, especially while parent birds are caring for their young. But the length of time the family groups stay together varies by bird. Some birds, such as the American Robin, pair for life and are very faithful to one nesting place: The same pair of robins may raise a brood every year in your yard. Others change mates several times a summer. And just as a human neighborhood may have 50 human families, a bird neighborhood may include 50 separate pairs of the same bird species, such as robins.

Territory

Do you have a special place that you call your own? Like humans, birds establish places that are "theirs." We call these places a bird's territory. There are no official pieces of paper, no fences or property lines to show bird territories. Instead, birds tell each other what places are theirs by using various signals: displays of feathers and color, call notes, songs.

Bird territories overlap much more than humans' do. While we humans share town commons, parks, lakes, and other parts of our neighborhoods, we don't often share our living space with anyone but our own families. Birds are different. For one thing, their territories are usually temporary. The boundaries change somewhat every year. And more than one bird species may share the same space peacefully because they use different parts of the space, prefer different foods, and are active at different times of day. Think of your human neighborhood: If everyone worked in the same place, left for work and school at the same time, and bought exactly the same foods at the same supermarket, there'd be a real traffic jam! Differences make human and bird neighborhoods work.

Finding a niche

People have many occupations and ways of living. So do birds. Scientists call birds' occupations their **niches.** A bird's niche is largely related to the food it needs. Some birds have a very exact niche, like the Yellow-bellied Sapsucker. As you might have guessed, the Sapsucker drills holes in trees to find sap. Others, like the American Robin, can find food almost anywhere at any time of year.

Share the Wealth
Even a small suburban yard may provide territory for several species of birds. Some look for nesting spots on or around buildings; others find that grass, flowers or shrubs harbor the insects they prefer. Bird feeders and nesting boxes are welcome extras, of course!

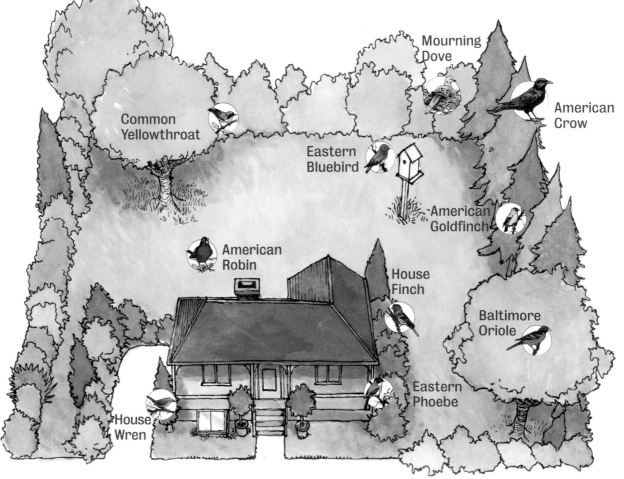

Mourning Dove

American Crow

Common Yellowthroat

Eastern Bluebird

American Goldfinch

American Robin

House Finch

Baltimore Oriole

Eastern Phoebe

House Wren

Ovenbird
Ground nest, 6–8" diameter

Whip-poor-will
Ground nest, 6–8"
diameter

Baltimore Oriole
Woven pendant nest,
8–10" long with a
4" diameter opening

White-breasted
Nuthatch
Cavity nest, hole
is 1¼" diameter and
cavity is 5–8" deep

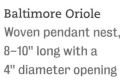

Nesting season

Birds build nests for several reasons: to hide, protect, and hatch their eggs, and to hold and provide a place to feed their young. A nest is like a nursery, bedroom, and dining room all in one, but there's one big difference between a nest and a house: no live-in adults. Parent birds might perch and roost around the nest area overnight, and some may spend days sitting on the nest to keep their eggs warm, but very few adult birds *live* in their nests.

Cavity nesters, like nuthatches, who use tree holes and human-made boxes for nesting, will roost in nest holes during bad weather. Adult birds usually find and eat food away from their nests, although when a pair is sitting on a nest, the non-sitting parent may bring food to the nest to feed its mate.

Lots of building styles

How hard do birds work to build a nest for their babies' comfort and protection? That depends on the bird. Whip-poor-wills just pile their eggs on the ground. Ovenbirds make basketlike ground

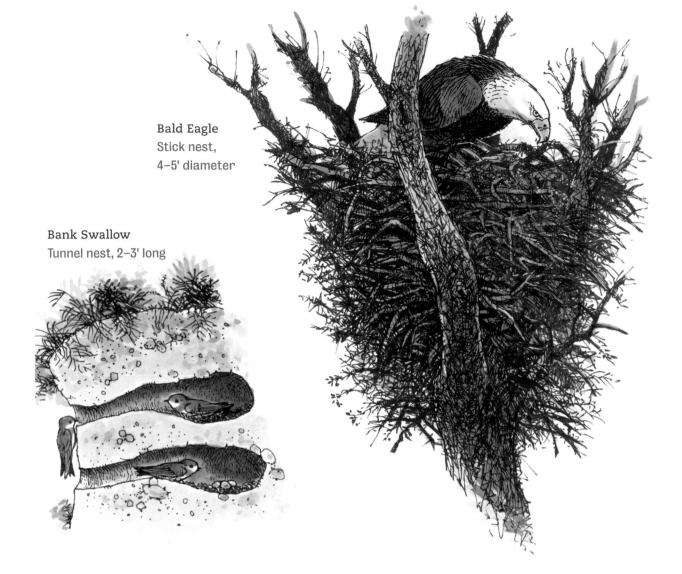

Bald Eagle
Stick nest,
4–5' diameter

Bank Swallow
Tunnel nest, 2–3' long

nests, while Bald Eagles craft gigantic, durable stick structures high in the trees. There are the underground tunnels of Bank Swallows, the complex, woven hammocks of Baltimore Orioles, and the Mourning Doves' few sticks on a flat branch. There are as many nest styles as there are bird species to build them.

Home Building
Each species has a different idea of the perfect nest.

Hide and seek

Birds have developed two main ways of keeping a nest secret from predators: **disguise** (looking like something they are not) and **camouflage** (blending in with something that's already there). The Ruby-throated Hummingbird, taking no chances, does both! It shapes its tiny nest to look like a knob on a branch, then decorates it with lichens and mosses to blend in with the tree limb.

Some birds, like the Common Nighthawk, take the easy approach to camouflage. They just lay their speckled eggs on a speckled surface, like a gravel roof or a rocky pond bed, and use no nest material at all!

Notes about nests

Birds use lots of different materials to build nests, including their own saliva, mud, spider webs, feathers, snake skins, animal fur, horsehair, and human-created items, like fishing line, ribbons, yarn, and paper. Birds get especially creative with plant materials, using fine fibers from plants like milkweed and coarse fibers from grapevines, as well as straw, pine needles, mosses, birch bark, and even flowers. Many bird nests have a layered structure, including a solid base, exterior camouflage, and interior lining. Nests may be remarkably delicate, intricate, and complex, containing more than a thousand pieces of material.

Will they nest here next year?

Most nests, especially those of the smaller songbirds, aren't reused the following year, although birds that have more than one brood may use the same nest during the same season. Building new nests every year may help limit bird parasites, and many songbird nests won't hold together through the stormy winter months.

Cavity-nesting birds may return to the same nest hole for several years. Many larger birds, like birds of prey or Great Blue Herons, will use the same nest for many years, placing new materials on top of the old. The results are bigger and bigger structures that may eventually weigh more than a ton.

The High Life
A Great Blue Heron's nest is usually 30 to 60 feet above ground.

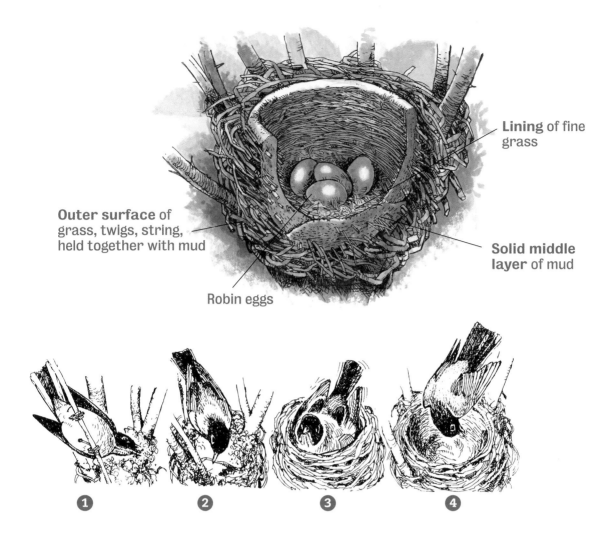

Lining of fine grass

Outer surface of grass, twigs, string, held together with mud

Solid middle layer of mud

Robin eggs

① ② ③ ④

How to Build a Nest
❶ The female robin collects grasses, ❷ forms the nest of grass and mud in a sheltered spot in a tree or building, ❸ creates a round form by stamping and squatting, and ❹ lines the nest with soft grass.

Slackers

A few birds don't build their own nests at all. Great Horned Owls get an early start on nesting in winter, using nests built the previous year by Great Blue Herons or Red-tailed Hawks. Brown-headed Cowbirds are the ultimate in hands-off parenting: They don't build nests *or* raise young. They simply lay an egg in another bird's nest and let another family raise the chick.

Housework and chores

Birds vary in the tidiness of their nests. Turkey Vulture nests receive little cleanup, but songbird nests are quite tidy. Waste products from the babies could attract predators, so parent birds remove it. "Yuck!" you might say, but it's easy to clean up: Baby songbirds' poop comes "pre-bagged" in a plasticlike **fecal sac,** which may be clear or white with a dark end. Often a parent bird may be seen bringing food to a nest, then leaving with a fecal sac carried in its beak. The sac is dropped at random well away from the nest.

Screech Owl's round egg

Baltimore Oriole's patterned egg

Ruby-throated Hummingbird's tiny egg

American Robin's pale blue egg

Trumpeter Swan's enormous egg

What's in an egg?

All birds lay eggs with a hard, calcium carbonate shell. And bird eggs all contain essentially the same things: undeveloped or unborn birds, yolk, and white, in various proportions.

You can tell immediately that a bird egg *is* an egg, yet they vary greatly in size, shape, color, pattern, and shell thickness. Even eggs from the same mother bird may look slightly different, and the number of eggs laid may be one or many. The time between laying and hatching might be two weeks or two months.

In North America the lightest birds, hummingbirds, lay the smallest eggs, and the heaviest birds, swans, lay the largest eggs. The relationship between egg size and parent size, however, is not always predictable. Smaller birds have relatively large eggs for their body size.

The best-laid plans

Most birds lay an egg a day until they have a **clutch,** which means the right number of eggs to incubate. During **incubation,** parent birds transfer warmth and moisture from their bodies to the eggs by gently sitting on them. Each bird species is a little different, so one species may stop laying when there are three eggs in the nest, and another won't stop until there are eight.

An egg which has just been laid can be "stored" in the nest for a week or so and doesn't need much besides a sheltered location and steady temperature and humidity. Once the birds start to sit on a completed clutch to incubate them, however, the eggs need almost constant attention. They must be turned every five to twenty minutes to prevent the inner contents from "sticking" to the side of the egg and developing unevenly. The eggs' temperature must be kept at between 96 and 100°F — not terribly hot, since birds' body - temperatures range from 100 to 113°F, but a challenge if the weather turns cool!

Occasionally, an egg doesn't hatch. Once all the other babies have hatched, a parent generally removes it from the nest to keep it from being broken and attracting predators.

Hatching time

Inside every egg is an embryonic baby bird that needs only warmth and moisture to incubate. What hatches from that egg? Is it a helpless, almost featherless tiny baby, or a speedy little lump of down that can run and hide? It could be either one!

Precocial hatchlings are incubated longer by their parents but hatch with their eyes open. They are born downy and ready to run, like baby chicks, or to swim, like baby ducks. They leave the nest within a day of hatching. Wild Turkeys, Ruffed Grouse, Killdeer, and many water and shorebirds all have precocial young.

When **altricial** hatchlings emerge, their eyes are closed, and they are naked and unable to walk. The nest holds them up. They hatch sooner than precocial babies do, but they need more time before they're ready to hop, run, and fly. They'll stay in their nest for two or three weeks. Robins, wrens, and swallows all have altricial young.

Focus on fledglings

Baby birds are called **nestlings** while in the nest. Young birds that have left their nests but are still dependent on their parents are called **fledglings.** Since most precocial birds leave their nests immediately, the term fledgling is usually reserved for altricial birds.

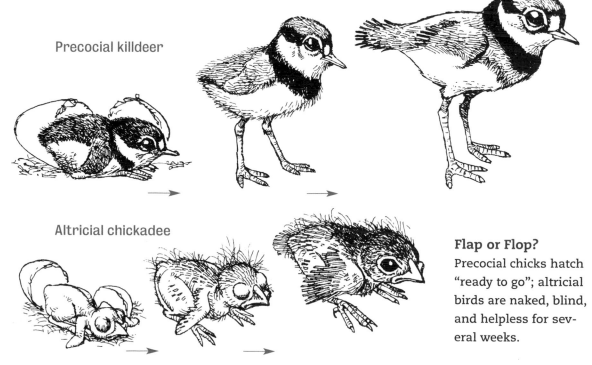

Precocial killdeer

Altricial chickadee

What's for Dinner?
Cedar Waxwing babies (*above*) are altricial; Common Terns (*opposite*) are precocial. But both depend on their parents for food for several weeks after birth.

Fledgling birds are at their most vulnerable stage of life. They may leave the nest able only to flutter and hop. Or they may take a short flight and land on the ground, unable to fly back into a shrub or tree. They attract a lot of attention with their struggles to fly, and often call actively for their parents to come and feed them. This makes fledglings very vulnerable to predators, such as cats.

To protect their babies, parent birds have to act aggressively. They may use **chip calls** (short, loud, one-syllable alarm notes) to warn fledglings when predators are around. Just like birds' songs, each bird species makes a particular chip call, and every bird has a

What a Birthday!

Wood Ducks nest in tree cavities or nest boxes, either in wetlands or as much as a mile from the water, between 3 and 50 feet above the water or ground. The nest is 2 feet deep and lined with down feathers. So imagine the precocial Wood Duck's first day on earth: Struggle out of your egg. Use your claws to climb the two feet up out of the nest to the entrance hole, then jump 50 feet to the ground (with your siblings behind you, pushing and shoving!). Once you're on the ground, walk maybe a mile to the water's edge, and learn to swim. So . . . what's on the agenda for Day Two?

6 a.m.: Hop out of nest and jump 50 ft. to ground

repertoire of four or five that mean different things, like "Danger: Keep quiet!", "Where are you? I'm here!", and so on. Jays, who care for their fledglings for three weeks, defend them vigorously from predators, even humans and cats, by flying around the intruder and pretending to attack.

Although fledgling birds may look smaller than adults, their bodies are almost full size. Their wing and tail feathers are short, still growing out from protective tubes. Those feathers stretch out just when their flight muscles are getting stronger. The fledglings will gradually begin to find or catch their own food.

6:15 a.m.: Walk up to a mile to water

8 a.m.: Learn to swim

A Budding Interest
Spring is a great time to
watch birds, such as this
Western Bluebird. The trees
are still leafless, making
the birds in them easier to
see, and many birds are
active and increasingly
vocal as the air warms up.

3

Thirty Birds to Know

Being aware of birds is a first step toward becoming a birder. You'll take your next strides by learning to recognize, and then to identify, some of the birds around you.

Start slowly. Remember that there are more than 800 bird species in North America alone, and it will take time and patience to get to know even a fraction of them.

Above all, enjoy your bird encounters. Spending half an hour watching a tiny, nameless bird hopping upside-down on a tree trunk will do more to improve your bird-watching skills than taking three seconds to say, "That's a robin!"

Questions to Ask before You Go

- **Where are you?** Far north, far south? Location is key.
- **What time of day is it?** Dawn and dusk may be best.
- **What's the habitat?** Forest, field, lake?
- **What season is it?** Bird activity levels vary with the seasons.
- **What's the local weather?** Weather can affect your ability to see birds.

Bird-watching tools

The only tools you really need to enjoy and learn about birds are your eyes, your ears, and your natural curiosity. We think a bird-watching journal and a pair of binoculars are two other great things to have, though, especially for beginners.

Journal basics

Your journal doesn't have to be fancy or expensive. We recommend a spiral-bound, 6 x 9-inch notebook filled with unlined paper. It should fold flat, so you can sketch and write in it easily while you stand outdoors. Find a pencil or pen, and you'll be ready to record what you see.

And what should you record in your journal? Well, that's really up to you. Some bird-watchers use the left-hand page to sketch and the right-hand page for notes. Others attach feathers, seeds, and other bird-related items right into their journals, identifying them later. Your journal should reflect you and your interests and record your bird-watching adventures in whatever way you want to remember them.

If you're not sure what to write in your journal, start simply. Describe what you see: "a big bird, a sky-blue bird, a bird the size of my shoe." Tell how you feel: "When it suddenly flew out it made my hair stand on end." What do you hear? "A sound like a squeaky gate, like my sister when I pinch her." Does a bird remind you of one you've seen before? Write that down, too. And don't forget the date, the time, where you were, and what the weather was like while you were out watching birds.

Did You Know?

You don't have to be totally quiet to watch birds, but you need to be able to listen for their songs and calls, their rustling and beak work. Lots of activity will scare them off, so be ready to sit or stand still for a good long time.

Focusing in

Binoculars (field glasses with strong lenses) can be quite useful to bird-watchers. There are many types available. Look at the diagram below to get a sense of how binoculars work and what they can do for you. Avoid the smallest, lightest binoculars: They're easy to handle, but they can be hard to use to locate birds.

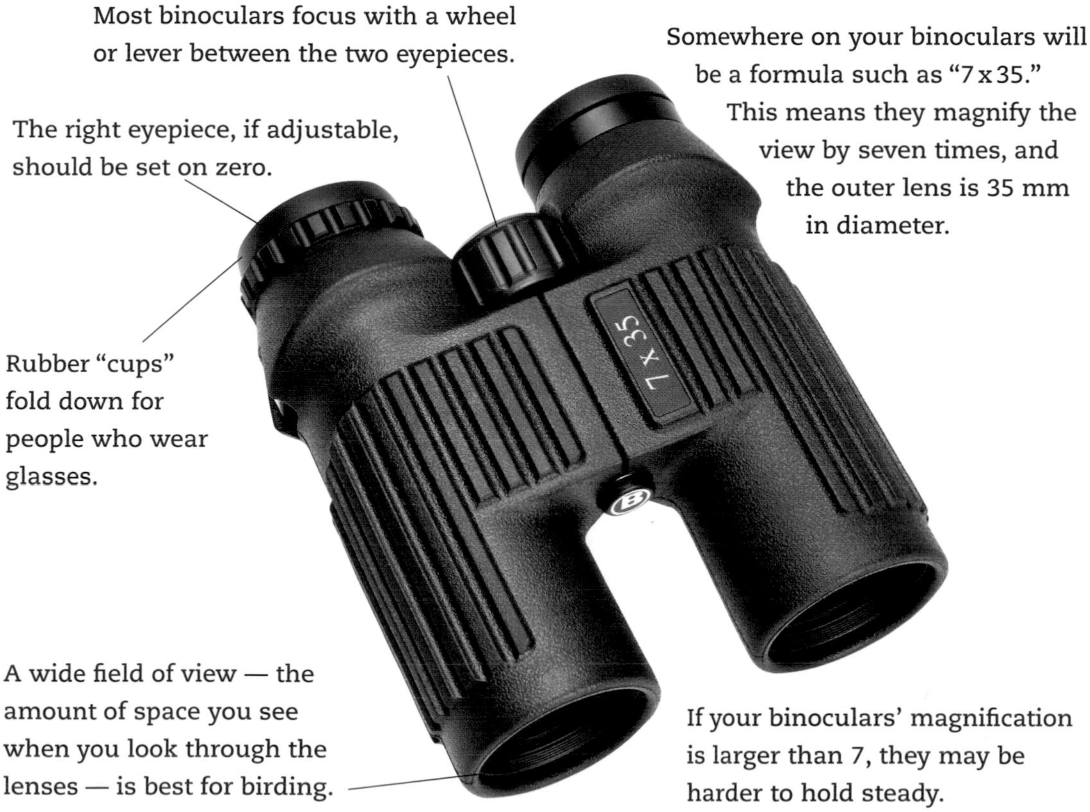

Most binoculars focus with a wheel or lever between the two eyepieces.

The right eyepiece, if adjustable, should be set on zero.

Somewhere on your binoculars will be a formula such as "7 x 35." This means they magnify the view by seven times, and the outer lens is 35 mm in diameter.

Rubber "cups" fold down for people who wear glasses.

A wide field of view — the amount of space you see when you look through the lenses — is best for birding.

If your binoculars' magnification is larger than 7, they may be harder to hold steady.

Different Ways of Using Binoculars

- Aim and focus at a general area *before* you look for a bird. You won't need much adjustment when the bird pops up.

- Keep your eyes aimed at the object you wish to see, then raise the binoculars to your eyes. Don't glance away!

- Note something unusual near the bird, find it, then slide your binoculars over to the bird.

- Practice focusing on stationary objects nearby and far away.

- With practice, you'll put your binoculars right on target every time without thinking.

Learning to recognize birds

Recognition is seeing a bird and knowing you've seen it before, or realizing that it's new and different. **Identification** is remembering or applying a name to it.

Identification takes practice and memorizing, and can be frustrating if you can't remember names easily. So concentrate on recognition first, and be assured that you can get great joy from bird-watching even if you can't identify a single bird!

There are four basic features to observe.

Color is one of the first things beginners notice. Overall color is the most obvious, but note also the color of eyelines (see chapter 1), stripes, spots, and patterns.

Can you see big differences among birds' shapes? Is the bird long and thin? Short and wide? Does it have a crest? What shape are its legs? Bill shape is another important clue: It can point you to a family of birds, such as sparrows or warblers.

Think about a bird's size in relation to the size of other birds you've seen. Is it bigger than a robin? Smaller than a chickadee? Remember that birds in flight have one set of silhouettes and sizes; birds at rest look different.

Birds' behavior can also tell you a lot. Many birds have unique ways of flying, hopping, or feeding. Nuthatches feed upside down; Eastern Phoebes and Palm Warblers wag their tails regularly; American Kestrels hover. Sometimes you'll recognize a bird with even a quick glance just because of its behavior.

Using the Identification Guide

The following pages are designed to help you identify 30 birds you may find all over North America, as well as a group of look-alikes. They're organized by color — black, gray, blue, red, orange, yellow, or brown. Start with the bird's color and then consider its size, bill type, and markings. The following pages also give you details about each bird's habitat, range, call or song, and some similar birds. At the end of the chapter you'll find a chart that describes where all 30 of these birds nest and what they eat.

Who Am I?
Study this bird's color, bill shape, size, and markings. Luckily for you, this one won't fly away, so take your time, then see if you can find it between page 44 and page 73.

Color:
Mostly gray, with black and white, warm tan, and subtle green

Habitat:
Near forest or in suburbs with plentiful trees

Bill shape:
short, pointy, strong-looking

Markings:
Black top of head, crisp white cheeks, black bib, tan underparts

Size:
Smaller than a robin, larger than a hummingbird

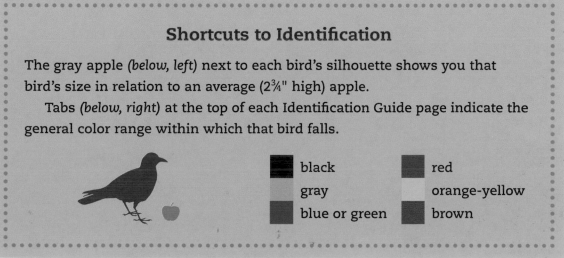

Shortcuts to Identification

The gray apple (*below, left*) next to each bird's silhouette shows you that bird's size in relation to an average (2¾" high) apple.

Tabs (*below, right*) at the top of each Identification Guide page indicate the general color range within which that bird falls.

black
gray
blue or green

red
orange-yellow
brown

Family: New World Vultures

Habitat: Soars over large areas of mixed habitats, from forests to deserts, wilderness to roadways

Call or song: Hisses and grunts, seldom heard except near nests and young

Size: 26–32" beak to tail

☐ Year round range

☐ Summer breeding range

Also meet:

California Condor

● A big vulture! **Nine-foot wingspan** (like two kids stretching out their arms) and broad wings, too

● Extinct in the wild in 1987, but **captive breeding** allowed birds to return to the wild

● Look for them in **California and Northern Arizona**

Turkey Vulture

Cathartes aura

To identify this big, soaring bird, look up at its wings and remember "V" for vulture. The Turkey Vulture, often called the buzzard, holds its wings tilted upward in a flattened V shape and seems to coast on the air. It soars in circles, often with a couple of other vultures for company. Seen up close, its head is naked and red and looks something like a turkey's. That's how it got its first name. The Turkey Vulture is one of our largest birds, and its favorite meal is anything dead. You're likely to see a Turkey Vulture in the middle of a highway, munching on road kill. These vultures nest in rock crevices, small caves, or hollow logs, and don't build or line the nest at all. In these well-hidden spots they'll raise two young vultures each year. When their young first fledge and fly, they have gray heads, unlike humans, whose heads are grayer as they get older!

Look again: Watch a soaring vulture and see how long it can maneuver in the wind without flapping its wings.

Family: Crows and Jays

Habitat: Adaptable to almost any habitat

Call or song: The famous "caw" is most often heard; also almost humanlike sounds

Size: 17½" beak to tail

☐ Year round range
☐ Winter range
☐ Summer breeding range

American Crow

Corvus brachyrhynchos

Who doesn't know the crow? Those big, black, glossy birds hang out somewhere in every neighborhood, sometimes in very large groups. And they know how to work together: Nesting groups share tasks, so one crow might serve as a guard while another finds food and a third keeps watch, turning attention away from a nest or giving an alarm. Crows probably understand their habitat and its opportunities better than any other animal. They find safety, shelter, food, and water in as many ways and places as you can imagine. Have you noticed how alert they are, always flying away just in time as a car approaches? They're quite intelligent, too: Crows can count, imitate the human voice, and remember information. They love bright things and will often carry objects away and hide them.

Look again: If you see crows feeding on the ground, look around for their "lookout" posted in a high tree. You'll probably hear its warning "Caw!" before you see it.

Also meet:

Common Raven

● **Less common** than the American Crow

● **Much bigger** and twice as heavy, with a croaky-cronky call

● Lives in **mountains and wilderness** areas

Family: Blackbirds

Habitat: Wet meadows, swamps, fields

Call or song: Gurgly and explosive "konk-a-ree!"

Size: 7½–9½" beak to tail

☐ Year round range

☐ Winter range

☐ Summer breeding range

Also meet:

Brewer's Blackbird

● Glossy, **purply-black**

● Commonly seen from **Midwest to West**

● Nests in **hay fields**; eats spilled grain on farms in winter

Red-winged Blackbird

Agelaius phoeniceus

Here's a bird that wants to be noticed. Like a bodybuilder showing off his tan, the male Red-winged Blackbird can often be found around bodies of water, flashing his fancy red shoulder patches for effect. The jet-black body and contrasting "epaulets" make the red-wing a colorful addition to his wetland habitat. The females are less colorful, but beautifully streaked, like giant sparrows. The longer, more pointed beak tells you they're blackbirds. And if you see a red-wing that's not as black as it should be, it's probably a first-year male. Their gurgly "konk-a reee" song can be loud. Look for the red-wing in stands of swamp cattails or in fields where feeding flocks gather during migration. The flocks are sometimes made up of more than one million birds.

Look again: Watch for migrating red-wings in late winter and notice that the males arrive first, often a month earlier than females, setting up their territories before courting season begins.

Family: Woodpeckers

Habitat: Forests and open woods

Call or song: Drumming on hollow branches; little "peek" calls and rattles

Size: 6¾–7" beak to tail

☐ Year round range

Downy Woodpecker

Picoides pubescens

These small woodpeckers are often mistaken for other kinds of birds until you notice their long, sturdy, pointed bills or their amazing hammering skills. From a resonant dead branch, tree trunk, or telephone pole, they loudly tell others that this is *their* territory. They also use that impressive bill for chiseling and chopping. Downy Woodpeckers are checkered black and white, with white backs and a little ketchup-red spot on the back of the male's head (and young birds' foreheads). They have big feet and use their tail as a prop, like a third leg, so they can hop easily up tree trunks to probe for insects. In winter you might see them in mixed flocks; in spring, both parents sit on their clutch of small white eggs, which hatch in less than two weeks.

Look again: Listen closely to find out where the Downy Woodpecker's hammering is coming from. Look high in trees and search the dead parts to see the downy's small form, parallel to the tree trunk.

Also meet:

Hairy Woodpecker

● **Larger** than the Downy Woodpecker; very similar markings

● **Shares space** with the downy

● **Beak** is about as long as its head; the downy's is shorter

Family: Blackbirds

Habitat: Swamps for nesting; meadows, feeders for feeding

Call or song: A hoarse "kerk"

Size: 11–13½" beak to tail

☐ Year round range
☐ Winter range
☐ Summer breeding range

Also meet:

Brown-headed Cowbird

● **Smaller than grackles**, with **shorter bills** and **brown heads**

● Often feeds with grackles and other blackbirds

● Female **lays 10 to 36 eggs each year** in the nests of other birds; all raised by other species

Common Grackle

Quiscalus quiscula

Have you ever met someone who'd eat anything? Well, meet another one: the Common Grackle. Offer fruit, grain, worms, mice, minnows, caterpillars, sunflower seeds, or salamanders, and the grackle won't turn up its beak! Maybe they're larger than typical blackbirds because of their willingness to chomp on any food that comes along. Their diet doesn't seem to hurt their looks, either: Their purplish heads are sleek; their large, wedge-shaped tails are long and sturdy. And with that iridescent (light-reflecting) body plumage, they sometimes look like walking rainbows. They're noisy, though, and some people don't welcome them, especially when they gather in large flocks to roost together. They'll come to feeders in large groups, too, so put out some cracked corn if you want to bring a party to your house. To watch them at their nest sites, look in wetlands and forest edges. They nest in groups, too — grackles like each other, and get together often!

Look again: Grackle tails are "keeled," or boat-shaped, with a downward "fold" in the middle. Note how often you see grackles around people's houses or other buildings: What do they seem to like most about humans?

Family: Starling and Myna Bird

Habitat: Everywhere and anywhere

Call or song: Sounds like humans talking, imitates other birds; sliding whistle sounds like a wolf-whistle

Size: 8½" beak to tail

☐ Year round range
☐ Summer breeding range

European Starling

Sturnus vulgaris

Just over a century ago, 100 of these birds were brought from Europe and set free for the first time in Central Park in New York City. They must have liked North America: The European Starling is now perhaps the most plentiful and common bird on the whole continent. It's also one of the most beautiful. The "starling" part of the name comes from the feathers they wear in winter, which are dotted with starry spots. By spring, the spots wear off the tips of the feathers, leaving unspangled breeding birds. If you live in a big city, you probably see starlings every day: They often build big colonies of nests on and around buildings. Although they're smaller than American Robins, European Starlings can be pushy, stealing nest boxes from other birds.

Look again: A starling flock in flight is a treat to watch. It moves like a school of fish, turning, banking, pulling to a stop, and changing direction all in unison, without ever colliding. Go out there and see for yourself!

Also meet:

Common Myna Bird

● Although not native to North America, a few escaped **Common Mynas survive in Florida**

● Chattering of **whistles, imitations, songs, and other vocals** will remind you of the European Starling, from the same family

● Go to **Africa** to see myna birds in real diversity

Family: Gulls and Terns

Habitat: Any area with available water: lakes, rivers, seashores

Call or song: Buglelike kewing and kawing calls

Size: 22–26" beak to tail

☐ Year round range
☐ Winter range
☐ Summer breeding range
☐ Migration range

Also meet:

Ring-billed Gull

● Smaller than a Herring Gull, with a **black ring around the bill** near the tip

● **Yellow feet**

● **Higher-pitched call** than the Herring Gull's

Herring Gull

Larus argentatus

You can always tell a gull by its outline: a large head, thick neck, and heavy bill. To identify a Herring Gull, look at its feet — they're pinkish — and check for a gray back and black wingtips. Gulls always seem to be doing something. They watch over shorelines for food opportunities, suddenly changing direction in mid-flight and plunging into a tide pool for a crab. Or they cruise around landfills and fast food restaurant dumpsters, begging humans for scraps. When they find shellfish, they drop them on parking lots or exposed rocks to break the shells and get at the meat inside. Herring Gulls are protective when nesting and make lots of body movements as they call loudly back and forth. There's a day's worth of watching in the activities of a single gull!

Look again: It takes four years and many feather molts for young gulls to develop adult colors and patterns. Look for a little red "target spot" on the adult gull's lower bill.

Family: **Mimic Thrushes**

Habitat: **Shrubby thickets,
edges of fields, farms, suburbs**

Call or song: **Imitates a
variety of sounds**

Size: **10" beak to tail**

☐ Year
round
range

☐ Summer
breeding
range

Northern Mockingbird

Mimus polyglottos

Who's that singing in the middle of the night? Chances are it's this long-tailed bird, especially if the moon is bright. And if he's not singing his own song, the Northern Mockingbird will happily sing the song of any other bird. He's a great mimic and easily imitates everything from insects to car alarms. Mockingbirds inhabit shrubby, dense thickets where they can find food and cover for their nests. You'll often see them thrashing around on the ground for fruits, their tails held out horizontally. Be aware during fledgling season: Mockingbirds can be aggressive around cats and other pets when their young are present. If you see large white patches on the wings and white outer tail feathers, you'll know that's a Northern Mockingbird in action!

Look again: Can you identify any of the other birds' songs that the Northern Mockingbird sings?

Also meet:

Gray Catbird

● Call note, "me-you!" **sounds like a cat**

● Can sing long strings of varied sounds with pauses

● Beautiful **reddish-brown undertail** feathers

● Similar shape to the Northern Mockingbird, but more uniformly gray with a black "cap" or crown

Tufted Titmouse

Family: Titmice, Verdins

Habitat: Forested areas, wood-lots, feeders (wet or dry)

Call or song: "Peer, peer, peer" and similar patterns of whistly notes

Size: 6½" beak to tail

☐ Year round range

Also meet:

Oak and Juniper Titmice

● These two birds were **once thought of as one species**

● Oak Titmouse appears from **western coastal areas to mid-California oak forests**

● Juniper Titmouse appears in **conifer areas** in the Southwest

● Almost pure light gray

Tufted Titmouse

Parus bicolor

In Scandinavian languages, "tit" means little. So the Tufted Titmouse's name really means "little mouse." Do you think it's just because this tiny bird is gray? Or is it perhaps because it moves quickly and is always busy? The Tufted Titmouse delights people all over the eastern half of the United States with its lively movements, bright black eyes, and expressive crest. It's one of the first birds to start to sing in late winter. And the titmouse is social, too: It's brave enough to stay fairly close to humans, and it nests in small groups and travels in flocks after nesting is over. You can easily attract titmice to nesting boxes and bird feeders in your yard. You might even have them eating out of your hand eventually! Because they don't migrate, titmice are active around feeders and in woodlands all year round. They probably mate for life.

Look again: Has the Tufted Titmouse been out in the rain too long? The next time you see one, look at how its cinnamon-colored flanks make it look as though the bird's wings are actually rusting.

Family: Flycatchers

Habitat: Open woodland near streams; farms, towns

Call or song: A burry "shree-brrr"

Size: 7" beak to tail

■ Year round range

■ Winter range

□ Summer breeding range

Eastern Phoebe

Sayornis phoebe

You can see from this photograph that the Eastern Phoebe is a little gray bird with a black beak. What you *can't* see, without going out to find a phoebe for yourself, is that it tips its tail continuously when it perches on a branch. This friendly flycatcher is at home near our homes, often nesting under overhangs, bridges, and in open sheds and other structures. Away from humans, Eastern Phoebes nest on rock faces and in crevices in giant boulders. They can be very tame near gardens; they may catch bugs right in front of your nose and dazzle you with their midair maneuvers. Eastern Phoebes were the first birds John James Audubon ever banded so that he could study their habits.

Look again: Phoebes don't bother to hide their nests, so they should be easy to find, right? Not always! Phoebes decorate their nests with camouflaging mosses. Sometimes the nest is hard to find even when you know it's there. Listen closely when you see an Eastern Phoebe in the open. Can you hear the pop of its beak when it catches an insect?

Also meet:

Say's Phoebe

● **Black-tailed**, with a **reddish belly**

● Replaces the Eastern Phoebe in **drier habitats west of the Rocky Mountains**

● Wags its tail, too!

Family: Herons, Egrets, Bitterns

Habitat: Wetlands, especially edges and shallows for feeding; swamps and beaver ponds with dead trees for nesting

Call or song: Loud, cranky, croaky sounds; one nickname for these birds is "big cranky," thanks to their voice

Size: 46–52" beak to tail

☐ Year round range
☐ Winter range
☐ Summer breeding range
☐ Migration range

Also meet:

Green Heron

● Much **smaller** than the Great Blue

● **Blue-green back** and **yellow-orange legs**

● **Shy**; prefers pond and stream edges

Great Blue Heron

Ardea herodias

Everything about Great Blue Herons is *long.* They are long-winged, long-necked, long-legged, and long-billed. They're graceful, too, whether flying with deep, slow wingbeats, stalking frogs and fish in shallow water, or even standing still, patiently waiting for prey to swim to them. They're not truly blue, but more of a bluish gray. When nesting, Great Blues work together, building large stick nests on dead trees. The males gather the nest materials while the females do the building. Their small colonies, called **rookeries**, can be found in wetlands.

Look again: In flight, Great Blue Herons are often mistaken for eagles due to their large wingspans. Look for long legs trailing behind and the "lump" in the throat area where the long neck folds up. That's a Great Blue!

Family: Nuthatches

Habitat: Forests, woodlands, patches of woods, suburbs and cities with enough trees

Call or song: Song is repeated soft notes; the "yer-yer-yer" song is the male's courting tune; calls include a nasal "yank" and other nasal sounds

Size: 5–6" beak to tail

☐ Year round range
☐ Winter range

White-breasted Nuthatch

Sitta carolinensis

This famous upside-down bird is a little acrobat and a familiar sight around backyard feeders. The White-breasted Nuthatch uses its long beak to probe from every possible angle for insects in tree bark. A Red-breasted Nuthatch is smaller, redder, with a black and white face, and prefers conifers. Nuthatches are fun to watch. They fan out and ruffle their wing and tail feathers. They hop up and down the trunks and limbs of trees, paying no attention to gravity. They are quite skilled at handling sunflower seeds: They twirl the seeds within their bills or grip them in their toes and hammer away at the seeds to open them. Nuthatches are cavity nesters, lining natural cracks or holes in trees with soft materials to hold their small whitish eggs. Nuthatches usually don't migrate.

Look again: Look at the size of a nuthatch's feet. They help with hopping and clinging to the underside of branches and limbs. But they are . . . well . . . big.

Also meet:

Brown Creeper

● Another **upside-down bird**

● Brown with a **downward-curved bill**

● Often works from the base of a tree upward in a spiral

Family: Ducks, Geese, and Swans

Habitat: Wetlands, ponds, open grassy areas, farmland

Call or song: Beautiful (and loud!) honking voices and calls can be heard when migrating

Size: 25–45" beak to tail

☐ Year round range

☐ Winter range

☐ Summer breeding range

Also meet:

Common Loon

● **Head is all black;** shorter neck than goose

● Known for its **spooky, laugh-like call**

● A **fish-eater**

● **Always on the water,** except when nesting or taking an early-morning flight

Canada Goose

Branta canadensis

All across North America, the Canada Goose is a familiar sight. Maybe you've spotted their V-shaped flocks flying in spring or fall, or heard their deep honking. On the ground, you'll recognize their white cheek patches and sleek black heads and necks. They're usually easy to view up close because they aren't really afraid of people, and they're attracted to parks, ponds, and public areas. Some geese don't migrate very far, if they live where unfrozen water is available all year. Others are far-north nesters who travel long distances to winter in the south.

Look again: If Canada Geese nest near you, look for their little families after the precocial yellow goslings hatch. Both parents guide the five or six young to the best grass for grazing. The parents look alike, but the males often guard the babies more aggressively, have thicker necks, and are slightly stouter.

Family: Chickadees and Titmice

Habitat: Forests, woodlots, suburbs with trees

Call or song: Clear "fee-bee" (territorial); other conversational phrases that sound like their name, such as "chick-a-dee-dee-dee"

Size: 5½" beak to tail

☐ Year round range

Black-capped Chickadee

Parus atricapillus

Friendly, curious, tame, and charming, Black-capped Chickadees are many people's favorite feeder birds. They're very talkative, even among themselves, making a variety of conversational sounds. It's easy to attract them, if you want to watch them at close range, by imitating their squeaks and "spishes." In the winter you'll see them in flocks with other birds, like woodpeckers and nuthatches, visiting bird feeders. When spring comes, the chickadees move into forested areas to nest. They'll often find a small, dead tree less than six feet tall and chisel a small hole in the soft wood. They line their nest hole with moss, plants, feathers, and fur. Chickadees are talented fliers: Note how fast they can change direction!

Look again: Black-capped Chickadees are curious. Put some natural objects near your bird feeders, such as strips of bark, plant galls, unusual seeds, nuts, or berries. Watch what the chickadees do. They'll actively examine, investigate, and probe the objects. Also watch for chickadees feeding upside down to reach insects and their larvae.

Also meet:

Carolina Chickadee

● Common in the **southeast United States**

● **Smaller** than the Black-capped Chickadee

● **Comes to feeders**

Family: Pigeons and Doves

Habitat: Cities and countryside; may inhabit areas with good nesting structures including cupolas on old barns, country town-hall belfry towers, bridges and overpasses, skyscrapers

Call or song: "Cooh, rooh, cooh"

Size: 13–14" beak to tail

Year round range

Also meet:

Mourning Dove

● Its name comes from its **beautiful, sad cooing** ("coo-EEE, cooh . . . cooh")

● Beautiful, **pointy, tapered tail and pointed wings** are obvious in flight

● **Pinkish tan** doves often seen at feeders in small flocks

Rock Pigeon

Columba livia

These birds were first used to carry messages in Roman times, and they were probably tamed more than six thousand years ago. Today's Rock Pigeons are the descendants of pigeons European settlers brought to North America in the early 1600s. Rock Pigeons have smallish heads that "bob" when they walk and fairly plump shapes. They are well adapted for walking on the ground: Have you seen them strolling around open spaces like city squares? They get quite used to humans in these habitats, eating bread and other offerings straight from people's hands. They often nest in high places on buildings. When not nesting, they are usually seen in groups. Rock Pigeons have beautiful iridescent feathers on their necks and backs in the area called the collar or mantle. They are surprisingly good fliers, capable of quick turns and flight speeds of more than 85 miles per hour.

Look again: Rock Pigeons come in many varieties of pattern and color. How many different color combinations can you find?

Family: Swallows

Habitat: Grasslands, marshes, open forests, lakes, rivers

Call or song: Lots of watery chittering and a beautiful little song of tweety notes

Size: 5¾" beak to tail

- Year round range
- Winter range
- Summer breeding range
- Migration range

Tree Swallow

Tachycineta bicolor

Most swallows are named for where they nest: tree, cliff, barn, or bank. But maybe they should be named for how they fly! Swallows are the most graceful and acrobatic fliers of the bird world, swooping and looping, with their beaks open to catch their insect meals. Bristles at the edges of their beaks help hold their prey in place. Recognize Tree Swallows by their beautiful blue upper bodies and pure white bellies and throats. First-year females are not blue, so if you see a pair with one blue and one grayish swallow, you're seeing a young female. After that first year, though, both males and females are blue and are hard to tell apart. A beaver pond is a great place to start looking for Tree Swallows: The water attracts insects, and the dead trees have plenty of good holes for nests. Swallows line their nests with feathers and lay white eggs, usually five or six in a clutch.

Look again: If you live near where Tree Swallows nest, put out multicolored feathers bought from a craft store. Watch the swallows pluck the feathers from the ground and the air to use for their nests.

Also meet:

Barn Swallow

- **Longer,** more **deeply forked tail** than the Tree Swallow

- Likes to **follow farm or garden equipment** to feed on insects

- Often **nests in the same place year after year,** usually on beams in barns

- **Reddish underneath**

Family: Hummingbirds

Habitat: Forests, woods, gardens, and farms

Call or song: Their humming is actually the flapping of their wings; they also make high-pitched sounds, mostly calls

Size: 3-3¾" beak to tail

☐ Winter range
☐ Summer breeding range
☐ Migration range

Also meet:

Anna's Hummingbird

● The most familiar garden hummer of the **West Coast**

● The **male has red throat** and crown or head

● Some **females have red spots on the throat**

Ruby-throated Hummingbird

Archilochus colubris

Red seems to be the Ruby-throated Hummingbird's favorite color: These tiny birds are attracted to red flowers and red plastic feeders most of all. They like flowers with long, tubelike blooms, such as petunias and bee balm, and they use their needle-thin bills to sip the nectar inside. Hummingbirds are colorful, full of energy, and skillful fliers. They can hover in one spot, their wings moving so fast that you won't be able to see them. They're also the only bird that can fly backwards! Plant the flowers they like, or set up hummingbird feeders, and watch how hummers chase away other birds and bees. They'll take over your yard, even flying right in your face if they choose. Good luck finding a hummingbird's nest, though: It's only about two inches across, just big enough to hold two pea-sized eggs.

Look again: In spring and summer, watch for the "pendulum display" of the male Ruby-throat: He flies back and forth in a long arc of about 50 feet, like a clock pendulum, while the female sits and watches.

Family: Crows and Jays

Habitat: Open forests, city parks, gardens

Call or song: Squawks, screams, rattles, and whistles; loud "Jay! Jay! Jay!"

Size: 11" beak to tail

Year round range

Winter range

Blue Jay

Cyanocitta cristata

If birds were kids, the Blue Jay would be the kid who's always in trouble with the teacher. Jays are "take charge" birds: noisy and pushy, with bold blue colors, large crests, and loud voices. But they're also very intelligent, with many social behaviors and activities. Like squirrels, Blue Jays store acorns in the ground for their winter feasts. They'll appear at feeders in large groups, but may nest in deep forests as well. Jays are clever about concealing their nests, using lichens and mosses for camouflage. The fledglings stay with their parents for many weeks. Jays have many voices. There's the familiar single-call, squeaky-wheel sound, but jays also sing a more musical song in early spring. They're also pretty good mimics: The Blue Jay's imitation of the Red-shouldered Hawk is especially true to life.

Look again: How many shades of blue do you see in a Blue Jay? Think about the colors in a paint box: Can you see Cerulean, cobalt, Prussian? Others?

Also meet:

Steller's Jay

● **Blackish crest and back**

● **Colors vary** from region to region

● **Inhabits the western third of the United States**, coming to feeders; **noisy and obvious**.

Thirty Birds to Know **61**

Family: Thrushes

Habitat: Open farmland, fields, and meadows

Call or song: Short, "cheery" musical phrases

Size: 7–7½" beak to tail

☐ Year round range

☐ Winter range

☐ Summer breeding range

Also meet:

Western Bluebird

- Males have **all-blue heads**
- **Bellies are gray,** not white
- They're **cavity nesters** that will nest in boxes

Eastern Bluebird

Sialia sialis

These farmland and orchard thrushes look like pieces of the sky with their blue, orange, gray, and white markings. Males have bright blue heads, wings and tails; females are more grayish, but have some blue in tails and wings. Sunset orange breasts contrast with cloud-white, gray, or even blue bellies. Eastern Bluebirds like to hunt in short grass from low perches. They take so well to bird houses in meadows that birders have created "bluebird trails," hundreds of human-made houses installed along a route, road, or trail. Even so, the Eastern Bluebird is always competing for nesting places with house sparrows and starlings. The number of Eastern Bluebirds east of the Rockies dropped sharply in the early twentieth century but is now steadily increasing again, with human help.

Look again: Wintering birds often feed on the red berry heads of sumac shrubs after late snowstorms, when ground hunting is not possible.

Family: Ducks, Geese, and Swans

Habitat: Marshes, ponds, lakes

Call or song: A loud quack that sounds just like "quack"!

Size: 23" beak to tail

☐ Year round range

☐ Winter range

☐ Summer breeding range

Mallard

Anas platyrhynchos

Mallards are one of the most colorful of our common birds. You can see them anywhere there is a pond of any size, even in city parks. They might seem tame, because of their gentle nature and expressive quacking, but they're much shyer in wilder habitats. Mallards feed by straining algae and duckweed, a very small floating plant, from the water surface through their bills. The males shed their lovely green head feathers and become drab for a few weeks in mid-summer during molting. Wherever many ducks gather together, you may see some that look a little like Mallards, but aren't quite right. That's because Mallard families combine with both American Black Ducks and domestic ducks. If Mallards are plentiful near you, watch them carefully. Can you tell the difference between males, females, juveniles, and "combination" ducks?

Also meet:

American Black Duck

● Look for **white wing linings** when they fly; **olive or greenish bill**

● Has bred with Mallard so much that **pure American Black Duck numbers are decreasing**

● **Threatened by lead shot** in wetlands

Look again: Have you seen Mallards upside down in the water? They're "dabbling." Dabbling is a way of feeding that lets the duck tip forward and reach deeply into the water and pond bottom without actually diving. Bottoms up!

Family: Cardinals, Buntings, and Grosbeaks

Habitat: Suburbs with trees and woodlots

Call or song: Loud, clear rhythmic "choit . . . choit . . . choit . . . chuchuchuchu" and "bir-dee, bir-dee, bir-dee"; more than 20 other songs

Size: 7½–9¼" beak to tail

Year round range

Also meet:

Scarlet Tanager

- Also **bright red**, but with **black wings**

- **No crest**

- **Sings from treetops** to find a mate

Northern Cardinal

Cardinalis cardinalis

Some birds just naturally look like royalty: The Northern Cardinal is one of those. Cardinals are almost fierce-looking, with large feather crests that make them look tall and powerful. They get their name from the Roman Catholic church: A cardinal is an important leader who wears bright red robes. The female cardinal's robes aren't as striking as the male's: They're olivey brown, with reddish tails and wings. But when it comes to singing, both male and female stand out! They sing all through the year, unlike most other birds, who do most of their singing in the spring. See that bulky reddish bill? It's built for crushing seeds, insects, and even snails. Cardinals like forest edges and backyards in suburban neighborhoods, and they will come to feeders at dawn and dusk for sunflower seeds. They raise more than one brood each year, often into late fall.

Look again: Male cardinals often tap fiercely at windows of houses. They see their reflection and think it's a competitor. If it's annoying, try soaping the window until the males get busy with hatched young!

Family: **Thrushes**

Habitat: **Everywhere and any-where, from old-growth forests to city backyards**

Call or song: **Musical quality, flutelike phrases and pauses ("Cheer-up, cheerily") delivered at dawn and dusk**

Size: **10" beak to tail**

☐ Year round range
☐ Winter range
☐ Summer breeding range

American Robin

Turdus migratorius

Maybe you've seen an American Robin hopping, or standing proudly, in a garden or park somewhere. If you have, you'll remember this beautiful bird with big eyes and a plump red breast. Robins are quite at home around people or in deep forests. They run about on lawns and seem to listen for prey, tipping their heads from side to side before suddenly dashing over and grabbing an (until then) invisible worm. Although many people think that the first robins mean the return of spring, these birds live year-round in all of the United States and summer in Canada. But they do have huge migrations in spring. Robins often build their nests in sheltered spots next to homes and in gardens and parks. They may raise three broods of nestlings in a year.

Look again: Can you see a difference in the color intensity of American Robins in a flock or in a pair? Females are exactly the same color and pattern but often paler than males.

Also meet:

Hermit Thrush

● Shaped like the American Robin, but **two shades of brown with a streaked breast**

● **Beautiful song** echoes from deep forests

● **Flicks its tail** a lot

Family: Finches

Habitat: Forests and woodlots; feeder areas in winter

Call or song: Beautiful, musical, warbly, and tuneful

Size: 5½–6¼" beak to tail

Year round range
Winter range
Summer breeding range
Migration range

Also meet:
....

House Finch

● **Known as a linnet** when introduced to New York in the 1940s

● **Nests close to houses**

● Especially tame; often **builds nests in potted plants**

● Orange-red, not purplish

Purple Finch

Carpodacus purpureus

It might take some time and practice before you can tell the difference between this bird and the House Finch, below. Both males and females of each species look quite a lot alike. These streaky reddish finches have some of the sweetest songs in the bird world, offered free of charge in your back-yard in late winter and spring. See that stout, seed-eating bill? It's typical of finches of all kinds. The Purple Finch is a frequent visitor at feeders and may be seen in winter with flocks of goldfinches, House Finches, and Pine Siskins. Purple Finches prefer to nest in forests and trees, especially in **coniferous** (cone-bearing) trees. They often line their nests with hair. The clearing of forested areas may be caus-ing a decline in the population of Purple Finches in the eastern United States. Watch the way they fly: They move forward with bursts of energy, pulling their wings tightly against their sides for a second after every few wing beats. Other finches and sparrows fly similarly.

Look again: To tell Purple Finches and House Finches apart, look for a bold, light line above the female Purple Finch's eye. The female House Finch doesn't have one. The male House Finch is orange-red; the male Purple Finch is purplish-red. And the male House Finch has streaked flanks, while the male Purple Finch is just reddish.

Family: Blackbirds

Habitat: Suburbs, forest edges, farmland

Call or song: Whistled phrases: "pee-per, pee-per. Powder, powder, peeper"

Size: 7-8¼" beak to tail

☐ Winter range
☐ Summer breeding range
☐ Migration range

Baltimore Oriole

Icterus galbula

These cheery orange and black birds are straight-line fliers: They beat their wings quickly, but their line of flight is clear and direct. Although medium-sized, Baltimore Orioles always seem to take on jobs that you'd expect smaller birds to do: clinging to apple blossoms and sipping their nectar, pecking at bark for tiny insects on small tree branches, and drinking rainwater from new leaves. They prefer the upper reaches of tall shade trees, where the females weave amazing nests from grass, hair, plant fibers, horse hair, string, and yarn. The finished nest hangs like a silvery bag from a tiny branch, sometimes as much as 60 feet above the ground. Use your binoculars if you go looking for one! Like many colorful birds, the female Baltimore Oriole's feathers are a duller orange than the male's.

Look again: Put out sliced oranges at feeders in spring to attract Baltimore Orioles. Watch your hummingbird feeder: Orioles will endure awkward positions to get at the nectar!

Also meet:

Bullock's Oriole

● **Larger white wing patch**

● **Orange on the face** instead of a black hood

● A **western species** that combines with Baltimore Orioles where their ranges overlap. Ornithologists once considered them the same species, the Northern Oriole

Family: Warblers

Habitat: Shrubby thickets

Call or song: "Sweet, sweet, sweet, where is my sweet?!"

Size: 5" beak to tail

☐ Year-round range
☐ Winter range
☐ Summer breeding range
☐ Migration range

Also meet:

Common Yellowthroat

● **Calls "Wich-i-ta, Wichita, Wichita!"** as if in answer to Yellow Warbler

● Both female and male have **yellow throats**

● Males' large **black mask** is eye-catching

Yellow Warbler

Dendroica petechia

Warblers are like butterflies: They come in lots of different colors and patterns and make their homes in every available habitat. And there are more than 50 species of warbler in North America. They're small (chickadee-sized) with short, pointy bills and short tails. Yellow Warblers live up to their names: They're almost completely yellow, except for cinnamon streaks on the breasts of males. They prefer shrubby countryside to dense forest and nest near the water of swamps or ponds. Brown-headed Cowbirds often choose to lay their eggs in Yellow Warblers' nests, hoping the warblers will bring the cowbirds up as their own. Sometimes they do, but sometimes the female Yellow Warbler seems to know what's going on. She'll build another nest right on top of the first one, ignoring the cowbird's egg (and any eggs she's laid herself), and lay a new clutch. Birders have found as many as six nests stacked on top of each other, each with a hated cowbird egg buried inside.

Look again: The Yellow Warbler will respond to "chips" and squeaks from humans and will often approach quite near. Kiss your palm to make these sounds.

Family: Finches

Habitat: Everywhere

Call or song: A complicated song like a canary's; calling in flight is distinctive, a "perchickoree"

Size: 5" beak to tail

☐ Year round range

☐ Winter range

☐ Summer breeding range

American Goldfinch

Carduelis tristis

If you ever thought you saw a darting ball of sunshine, it was probably an American Goldfinch. Lots of these friendly little black and yellow birds can be seen year-round in gardens and at feeders. Goldfinches are expert at using their short, wide beaks to pry seeds out of tight places. They often begin with dandelions in spring, deftly pulling the winged seeds from the heads and even chasing the seeds as they drift in the air. Males in breeding season are bright yellow with black foreheads and wings. Females are a duller yellowish-gray. Although the birds seem to be active and courting in spring, they wait until late summer to actually nest, taking advantage of the ample seeds to feed their young. Goldfinch nests are carefully woven of grasses and other vegetation, with plenty of plant down as a lining. Along with their bright yellow feathers, also notice the American Goldfinch's roller-coaster way of flying.

Look again: The American Goldfinch's plumage gradually brightens from late winter to late summer. Watch for it to turn bright yellow. Spring isn't far away!

Also meet:

Evening Grosbeak

● Similarly colored, **larger, bulkier bird**

● **Enormous beak,** (*gros* means "big" or "fat" in French)

● Males have **yellow foreheads**

Family: Owls

Habitat: Many habitats, including desert, forest, swamp, cities

Call or song: "Who . . . who-who-who. . . who-ooo-oo" is deep and low, carrying far away but never loud

Size: 18–25" beak to tail

☐ Year round range

Also meet:

Screech-Owl (Eastern & Western)

● Because of **ear tufts or horns,** often misidentified as baby Great Horned Owls

● **Yellow-eyed** and fearless

● **Mournful call**

Great Horned Owl

Bubo virginianus

The "horns" on the Great Horned Owl's head can't hurt you: They're really just tufts of feathers, and are probably the softest horns you'll find on any animal. But they help make this large, stout bird look wise and alert. Great Horned Owls are wide-ranging birds, found from the northern Arctic to the southern tip of South America. These owls "borrow" (or is it steal?) the nests of other birds, including Red-tailed Hawks' and Great Blue Herons', and lay their whitish eggs in them. Maybe that's why they start nesting so early. They're powerful hunters who can attack animals that are bigger and heavier than they are. They're also protective parents who aren't afraid of chasing even humans away from their young. Will you ever see one during the day? Yes, sometimes, although they are most active at dusk. Don't expect to hear the sound of their wings, though: They're silent fliers.

Look again: Go out and listen! Great Horned Owls are early nesters, so their hoots may often be heard in late February near wetland forests. Fledglings follow their parents for more than six months and emit a "sneaker screech" sound to encourage parents to come and feed them.

Family: Hawk Family, Eagles, Hawks, Kites

Habitat: Forest edges, grasslands, desert

Call or song: A loud "Screee!", usually when soaring

Size: 19–25" beak to tail

□ Year round range
□ Winter range
□ Summer breeding range

Red-tailed Hawk

Buteo jamaicensis

Are you going on a long car trip anytime soon? Watch the edges of the highway, especially the trees and open sky over the road. If you see a big bird perched or flying there, it's probably a Red-tailed Hawk, waiting for rabbits and other prey. You can see the chestnut tail color best on adult birds from above. This hawk, like several other raptors, soars using a few strong beats of its wings, then a long glide. When watching a soaring large bird, wait for it to angle toward you, so that the top of its tail is visible. You may see a flash of red even without binoculars. The Red-tail catches animals alive and takes them away to a perch to eat them. Its strong hooked beak is designed to tear food, and its sharp talons hold prey tightly.

Look again: Many bird-watchers quickly identify Red-tails by their darker feathers in the tummy area, called a belly band.

Also meet:

American Kestrel

● A falcon rather than a hawk; has **pointy wings** and **hovers in mid-air**

● Also seen frequently **along highways**

● **More colorful** than the Red-tailed Hawk, with a **reddish back** and **blue-gray wings**

Family: Sparrows

Habitat: Brushy thickets

Call or song: "Sweet, sweet, sweet . . ." beginning every song

Size: 5¾–7½" beak to tail

☐ Year round range

☐ Winter range

☐ Summer breeding range

Also meet:

Chipping Sparrow

● **Smaller,** with **chestnut cap** on top of head; **plain breast,** without streaks

● **Song is a monotonous trill** from tall pines and spruces

● **Will use animal hair for lining nests,** collecting it right from your horse or other pets

Song Sparrow

Melospiza melodia

You can find some kind of sparrow on any continent in the world except Antarctica. They're adaptable birds and they quickly figure out how to use human activities, like farming, for their own survival. The Song Sparrow is one of the most common and familiar birds of North America. It probably got its name because of its habit of sitting out in the open, singing loudly and happily to announce its territory. These brownish birds have streaked breasts with a central "spot" and short, cone-shaped bills, perfect for cracking the seeds they love. Song Sparrows often feed on the ground, sometimes scratching with their claws to find insects. They like shrubby edges and will readily make their homes in city parks and suburban gardens. You can often see Song Sparrows chasing other birds from their territory, although several species of sparrow might share a large backyard area.

Look again: The next time you see a Song Sparrow, notice how it flicks its long, rounded tail up and down as it flies.

Family: Wrens

Habitat: Shrubby edges of fields and forests

Call or song: Bubbling and explosive "chittly oodly" song

Size: 4¾" beak to tail

■ Year round range
■ Winter range
□ Summer breeding range
□ Migration range

House Wren

Troglodytes aedon

House Wrens are like tiny brown firecrackers with bent-up tails, always busy building multiple nests, chasing other birds, hunting insects from ground to tree limb. Every home should have a wren for good luck and natural insect control. Luckily, House Wrens will make their nests in cars or tractors, old buildings, pails, boxes, or hanging plant baskets without fear. To keep predators guessing, the males build many stick nests just before nesting season begins. Once they've found a mate, the female chooses her favorite stick nest and finishes it herself, lining it with soft materials.

Look again: Will House Wrens sing in a total downpour? Yes, House Wrens love rain.

Also meet:

Bewick's Wren

● A little **larger than the House Wren**

● **White line above eye**

● Often **seen in yards and at feeders in the west and southwest**

Where Birds Nest and What They Eat

Bird	Page	Nest	Food
Turkey Vulture	44	The bare ground of rocky cliff areas	Dead animals, large and small
American Crow	45	Sticks in large trees, often pines	Everything and anything, animal and vegetable, from highway carrion to tiny seeds; comes to feeders for corn bread
Red-winged Blackbird	46	A loose cup or bag hung from low vegetation on or near water	Seeds, grains, insects; comes to feeders
Downy Woodpecker	47	Holes, either made or found, in dead trees	Insects from tree trunks, limbs, and branches; comes to feeders for suet
Common Grackle	48	Big masses of vegetation, often near the ground; in colonies	Insects and seeds on ground; comes to feeders
European Starling	49	Tree cavities, holes in buildings, and nest boxes of other birds	Insects and seeds on ground; comes to feeders
Herring Gull	50	Seaweed, grass, or weeds on the ground on isolated islands in large bodies of water	Almost anything it can scavenge or catch live from shorelines, landfills
Northern Mockingbird	51	Cup-shaped, in shrubs	Larger insects as well as fruits and berries of many shrubs, especially in winter
Tufted Titmouse	52	Natural tree cavities or borrowed woodpecker holes	Seeds, berries, and insects, especially caterpillars; comes to feeders
Eastern Phoebe	53	A beautiful cup shape on a beam or ledge	Flying insects of many kinds: dragonflies, butterflies, flying ants
Great Blue Heron	54	Large stick nests on dead trees in small colonies	Frogs, fish, snakes and other water life, caught live from wetlands of all types and sizes, both fresh and salt water
White-breasted Nuthatch	55	Natural holes up high in trees	Insects probed from tree bark; comes to feeders
Canada Goose	56	Plant materials on ground near water; lined with down	Pond-edge vegetation, seeds in farm fields
Black-capped Chickadee	57	Tree cavities	Seeds, berries, fruits, small insect eggs and larvae; comes to feeders

Bird	Page	Nest	Food
Rock Pigeon	58	A few sticks in a platformlike nest on a horizontal surface such as a ledge, gutter, or cliff	Seeds at feeders; seeds and nuts in the wild
Tree Swallow	59	Holes in dead trees	Flying insects, caught as the swallow flies
Ruby-throated Hummingbird	60	A carefully camouflaged bump on a branch; very tiny cup	Nectar and insects; comes to special hummingbird feeders
Blue Jay	61	Bulky, loose, twig and vegetation nests in trees	Almost anything: nuts (including acorns), seeds, berries, insects, even carrion and other birds' young and eggs; comes to feeders
Eastern Bluebird	62	Tree cavities and nestboxes	Many kinds of insects and berries; comes to special feeders with mealworms
Mallard	63	Reeds and grasses, lined with feather down, in a depression near water in tall grass or herbaceous vegetation	Small seeds of aquatic plants and small water life; farm crops in fields
Northern Cardinal	64	Bowl-shaped nests of vegetation in shrubs	Insects, berries, seeds; comes to feeders
American Robin	65	Heavy, mud-strengthened bowl nests in trees and shrubs	Berries, insects, worms
Purple Finch	66	Grasses and twigs, cuplike	Seeds and insects; comes to feeders
Baltimore Oriole	67	Hanging, well-woven pouch in large trees	Fruit, flower nectar, insects, berries; comes to hummingbird feeders
Yellow Warbler	68	Cuplike, hidden in shrubs	Insects gleaned from shrubs
American Goldfinch	69	Thick-walled cup made of fine plant fibers in shrubs or small trees	Wild seeds in season; comes to feeders
Great Horned Owl	70	Large stick structures placed high off the ground in trees; usually borrowed	Small mammals, other birds including ducks, hawks, and other owls; even skunks!
Red-tailed Hawk	71	Bulky stick nests built high in very tall trees, near the trunk	Mice, rats, weasels, rabbits, pheasants, snakes
Song Sparrow	72	Cup-shaped, in shrubs	Seeds and insects on the ground; comes to feeders
House Wren	73	Cavity nesters, in any kind of cavity	Insects

4

The Wider World
of Birds

In this book, you'll see only a fraction of the birds that are actually out there in the world. We've shown you profiles of about 75; there are between 9,500 and 10,000 species of birds worldwide.

If that sounds like a lot, consider that scientists calculate the total number of different, known, living things on earth (including insects, mammals, snakes, fungi, turtles, and so on) to be around one and a half million (1,500,000). Some estimate that there may be more like 10 million

How Safe Are They?

Here is the percentage of the world's birds that are endangered.

- Birds that are not threatened, reasonably safe, stable
- Proven to be endangered or threatened, vulnerable
- Critical or entirely dependent on conservation

Note that nearly a quarter of all birds are in danger of becoming extinct.

8%

16%

76%

species, since remote places may harbor many more that have never been discovered. That makes birds look like a pretty small part of a very big picture.

But it's a complicated picture, and the well-being of one species, no matter how small, can have a significant impact on the well-being of many others. It makes good global sense to pay attention to how birds are thriving, both close to home and around the world.

Birds and biodiversity

Why is it important that there are so many bird species in the world? Does it really matter? Will it change your bird-watching experience? Here's what we think.

The big picture

Lots of people who care about nature want to understand how the many species on earth depend on each other. They're concerned about maintaining **biodiversity,** the dazzling variety of life on earth. That variety includes all species and habitats combined, and every little piece is a priceless part of the whole picture. As human activities destroy habitat and change climate, some of the earth's species may be lost before we even discover that they exist. And when a species is lost, near you or far away, other species can be affected.

The power of one

But what can a single person do to help preserve biodiversity? More than you think! Even one person studying, enjoying, and understanding just one species can make a difference. Studying the birds around you will make you a better citizen of the earth, and a better friend to all life. This chapter will tell you more about birds as a group, how they're studied, how they're threatened, and what makes them so fascinating.

Can you count?

We can make pretty good guesses about how many birds and bird species there are because of a simple activity: People count them. All over North America, local bird-watchers gather to record the birds they see or hear. A record like this is called a **census**. Bird censuses can measure both **diversity** (the number of bird *species*) and **abundance** (the number of individual birds *within a species*). These numbers are important to bird lovers and can be helpful to many others as well.

Did You Know?

Estimates suggest that there are more than 100 billion birds on earth, and at least 5 billion just in the United States. Try imagining that as a flock!

A good bird census helps answer two main questions: "How many different kinds of birds can we see in our area?" and "How many of each species can we see?" In your town, bird-watchers might be able to find 50 different species and count 9,000 Red-winged Blackbirds. Those are measures of diversity and abundance.

If you help with a bird census, you'll be contributing to science without having to be a scientist yourself. Every year, volunteers count birds in the same places during the same weeks. In summer, they do breeding censuses; in winter, it's called the Christmas Count. Scientists compare years of Christmas Counts and Breeding Season Censuses to track the number of birds in a species and find out whether the numbers are going up or going down.

Most Abundant, Now Extinct

The Passenger Pigeon once lived in eastern North America in *huge* numbers. It might have been the most abundant species in human history. Eyewitness accounts from the 1600s, 1700s, and 1800s reporting on Passenger Pigeon flocks help us imagine what billions of birds must have looked like. In 1625, one Manhattan settler described flocks "so numerous that they shut out the sunshine." An ornithologist in the early 1800s tried to count the birds, and came up with more than *two billion* birds in a single flock. Others walked for miles to measure the space taken up by one colony of nests in the treetops.

But Passenger Pigeons were also tasty. Hunters killed millions from a single colony in a single season, then shipped them to city markets to be sold for food. Almost 15 million came from one Wisconsin town alone.

As settlers moved west in the mid-1800s, they cut down the forests that supplied the pigeons with acorns and beechnuts. Hunting was outlawed gradually in the late 1800s, but these pigeons could feed, breed, and nest only in large groups. Once their numbers were reduced, they could not survive.

The last wild Passenger Pigeon was seen in 1900. And Martha, the last bird of her species, died in a zoo in 1914.

Some are common, some are rare

Solitary vs. Sociable

A California Condor *(top)* scans a large wilderness area alone, looking for carrion, while a male Northern Cardinal *(bottom)* may find plentiful meals by flitting the small distance from one shrubby yard to another.

You've probably noticed that you see some kinds of birds often, and others only once in a while. How often you see particular birds, and the number you see at one time, depends on what those birds eat, the kind of landscape they prefer, and the distance they have to travel to find what they need.

For example, the California Condor is a **scavenger:** It feeds on dead meat. Condors may have to search a large area in the dry, open landscape they inhabit for an animal that has died. There might be only one or two California Condors in a whole mountain range.

The Northern Cardinal, however, depends on flowering trees and shrubs and rarely has to travel far to find them. A typical neighborhood in the eastern United States might be home to fifty Northern Cardinals. The number of birds of the same species that live in a certain area is called its **density.**

Our birds, your birds

As you think about where birds live and how to find them, don't forget that large numbers of birds are on the move twice a year. Many of the birds we think of as "ours" spend their breeding season with us in North America and their winters in Central and South America. Their movement from north to south and back again is known as migration.

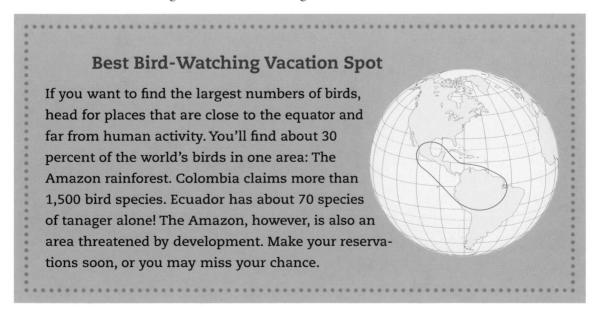

Best Bird-Watching Vacation Spot

If you want to find the largest numbers of birds, head for places that are close to the equator and far from human activity. You'll find about 30 percent of the world's birds in one area: The Amazon rainforest. Colombia claims more than 1,500 bird species. Ecuador has about 70 species of tanager alone! The Amazon, however, is also an area threatened by development. Make your reservations soon, or you may miss your chance.

Migration

Imagine flying just above the treetops in the dark at more than 30 miles per hour. Or coasting, thousands of feet in the air, with no map and no close-up view of what's around you. How do you cross the ocean and end up at exactly the right place, without any landmarks to follow except the waves? If you're a bird, this isn't a miracle: It's just everyday life!

To migrate means to move a long distance, generally as part of a flock or a loose group of others of the same species. True migration happens regularly, every year. It can happen during the day or at night, either along coastlines or on much-traveled routes called **flyways** across continents. Some birds migrate only a few hundred miles; others cover more than 30,000 miles and feed along the way. Songbirds fly low in migration, just above the treetops, while other birds, like geese, can be glimpsed from the windows of high-flying jets.

Birds are not the only creatures that migrate. Some mammals, like bats, also migrate, and so do some insects, including dragonflies and butterflies. You don't even have to fly to migrate: A few of our mammals, including caribou, make their journeys on foot. And don't forget whales, who get to swim and stay cool for their whole trip, while the birds sweat it out above them.

Q: How Do Birds Navigate?

A: We don't know exactly how birds find their way during migration. Scientists think that birds "see" the natural landmarks and landforms around where they live, and fit them to some kind of map in their brains. To cover the large distances between their winter and summer homes, birds also use the position of the sun, moon, and stars to find their way. On cloudy days, the patterns of light in the sky may be enough for them to steer by. And they're probably even able to follow the magnetic field of the earth.

One bird's migration story

You've just doubled your body weight in two weeks. No, it's not all those holiday desserts! You're a Blackpoll Warbler, and you're preparing to leave town under your own power.

If you were human, you might need to build muscle and *lose* weight to make it through an 85-hour, self-powered flight across the Atlantic Ocean. But you're a bird, and you've kept in good shape by flying around all summer. Extra fat helps power your muscles. So now you're ready to fly from Nova Scotia to Venezuela. You'll arrive at less than your normal body weight, and *very* hungry. Migration is the greatest weight-loss plan on earth!

And when spring comes to Nova Scotia, you'll turn around and make that long journey back there again. Why? Probably because there are lots of other birds sharing the lovely food and warm habitat in the tropics. If you fly back north, you'll find good summer feasts and more choice nesting spots than you would if you stayed in Venezuela. That's why you and 350 other species keep migrating, year after year.

And they're off! Migrating terns fly in relatively close formation as they travel from their summer homes in Canada and New England to South America.

Blackpoll Warbler

Birds in danger

If you love the idea of discovery, you'll be happy to hear this: People "find" about three new bird species every year, somewhere in the world. But we're in danger of losing more bird species every year than we discover.

Beware: extinction happens today

You probably know that dinosaurs are extinct, and that they died out long ago. But creatures from more recent times have also become extinct. And several other species are in danger of extinction right now, in North America and around the world.

Dinosaurs probably died out because of a major climate change. But we've lost the Dodo, Great Auk, and Passenger Pigeon within the last 350 years. The California Condor, Ivory-billed Woodpecker, and Whooping Crane are close to extinction now, too. Human actions, such as over-hunting, destroying habitat, and using pesticides and other chemicals, have killed off these birds or put them in danger.

Protecting our birds

Birds whose populations are very low, or going down fast, are considered **endangered.** Various laws have been made to protect them. The Endangered Species Act in the United States is a country-wide effort to save endangered birds like the Bald Eagle.

Already Gone

Five birds have become extinct in mainland North America in the past 150 years.

Each has a different story. Some were lost before humans could act, others could not be saved no matter how hard we tried. The lesson is that any bird can become extinct if we don't take action. To save birds, we must keep track of them and protect their populations.

Great Auk
extinct in 1844

Labrador Duck
extinct in 1875

It's just one law, but it keeps endangered species safe from chemicals, from hunting, and from having their habitats changed.

The Endangered Species Act has been successful, and it has encouraged some American states and Canadian provinces to adopt similar local laws. Meanwhile, other countries around the world have started endangered species lists as well. About 1,000 species of birds around the world are endangered in some way.

What's causing the problem?

One hundred years ago, the main threats to birds in the United States were over-hunting and clearing of forests. Now habitat loss is the main reason bird species are endangered. States like Massachusetts, once cleared for farms, are now mostly forested. The remaining farmland is being sold for house construction as the population spreads out. Because of these trends, many grassland birds — species that require fields, meadows, and other grassy places — are endangered in Massachusetts and other eastern states.

And habitat isn't being lost only in North America. Birds that migrate to the south face habitat loss on their wintering grounds. Migrating birds need forests and other habitats in Central and South America, which are disappearing at a rapid rate.

In addition to habitat loss, millions of birds are killed every year by house cats and by collisions with vehicles and buildings.

Worried? Well, we all should be! The next chapter tells how you can help.

Did You Know?
Some ornithologists try to raise endangered bird babies in captivity, without human contact. Birdlike puppets feed the babies and teach survival skills. The birds are returned to their natural habitat when they're ready to fledge.

Passenger Pigeon
extinct in 1914

Heath Hen
extinct in 1932

Carolina Parakeet
extinct in 1900

Just Hanging Out Birds, like this Black-capped Chickadee, will come to almost any feeder. For the birds' safety, make sure it is well-drained, protected from the weather, and made of materials that pose no hazards.

5

Birds and You

You can't keep birds from colliding with cars or cell towers, and you can't always stop the actions of cats or bulldozers. But there are a number of things you can do, right now, that will make a difference in the lives of birds.

No matter where you live in North America, the birds around you need places to live. You can help protect habitat and provide safe nesting spots for both migrant and year-round local birds. Even watching birds and making notes can make an important contribution to their survival.

Making Your Backyard Safe for Birds

If you have a backyard:

- plant a variety of trees and shrubs for perching and nesting
- set up feeding stations around the yard
- make a four-season bird arbor (see page 96)
- build or buy nesting boxes (see pages 98 and 99)
- provide clean water for bathing and drinking
- keep your cats in the house

If you don't have a backyard:

- set up a feeding station in a window or on a balcony
- provide perching places and clean water
- seek permission to put nest boxes in a park or on a rooftop

Balcony feeding station

A bird's schedule

Birds have routines just like you do. They have predictable daily, weekly, monthly, and yearly schedules. And just as your schedule changes sometimes, a bird's schedule might change because of day length, weather, ocean tides, ripening fruit, insect hatches, plants in bloom, or the presence of predators.

You can learn the schedules of birds in your neighborhood. Which birds wake up first? What are they doing in early April? In late September? You might have the very first bluebird of spring in your area, or the last fox sparrow in November. It's fun to keep a bird calendar to help you keep track of all these events.

Your calendar of bird happenings will look different from everyone else's, because you'll build it from your own observations. If you can get a friend to do one as well, you'll have a great time comparing notes. Once you've kept your calendar for a year, the fun really begins. You'll be ready the second year, wondering whether things will happen again in the same way. By the third year, people will be coming to you with questions like: Where are the Robins? Isn't this early for the Red-winged Blackbirds?

1. Migrant arrival dates. For males and females that you can easily tell apart, look for separate arrivals. For example, Red-winged Blackbird males arrive almost a month before females in some areas, setting up territories to prepare for their future mates.

2. First-song dates. This is a good winter observation, as resident birds often begin to sing and set up territories before migrants even get there.

3. Abundance numbers for one species of bird. For example, choose a day of the week and a time of day, and note how many American Goldfinches you see at your feeder or near your house at that time. The next week, look for goldfinches on that same day and at that same time. Do this throughout the year, and then graph your findings. When are goldfinches most abundant?

4. Feeder schedule. Who arrives first? At what time of day?

Did You Know?

Cats kill millions of songbirds each year, which makes them one of the biggest threats of all to birds. If you have a cat, don't attract birds to your neighborhood and then make them targets. Instead, turn your cat into an indoor couch potato. An indoor life will keep Kitty safe from wild predators, diseases, and parasites.

Your observations can also help protect birds. If you report what you notice to the local bird club, you'll help others understand and be aware of the activities of birds in your area. Even something as simple as waiting two weeks before beginning tree-cutting work in your neighborhood could make all the difference to migrating birds seeking shelter. Your notes could help others make that decision.

Here are the kinds of observations you might want to record on a bird calendar. Keep all your calendars: Comparing one year with another is fascinating.

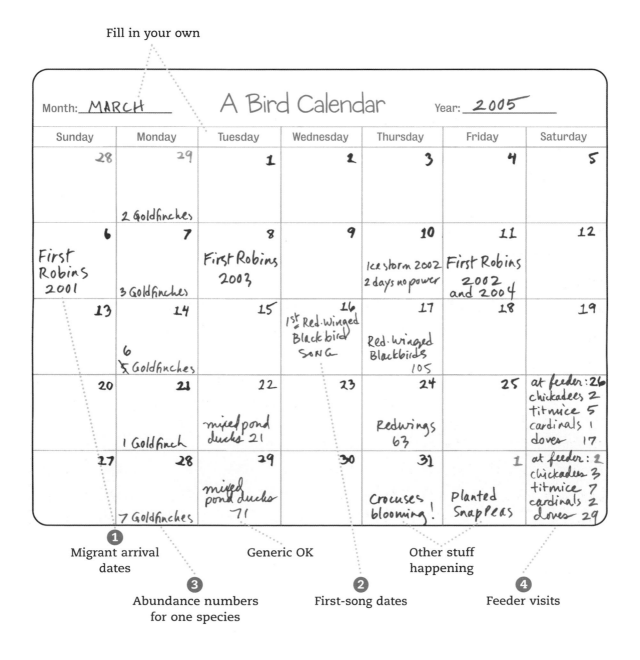

Fill in your own

Month: MARCH   A Bird Calendar   Year: 2005

Sunday	Monday	Tuesday	Wednesday	Thursday	Friday	Saturday
28	29 2 Goldfinches	1	2	3	4	5
6 First Robins 2001	7 3 Goldfinches	8 First Robins 2003	9	10 Ice storm 2002 2 days no power	11 First Robins 2002 and 2004	12
13	14 6 5 Goldfinches	15	16 1st Red-Winged Blackbird SONG	17 Red-Winged Blackbirds 105	18	19
20	21 1 Goldfinch	22 mixed pond ducks 21	23	24 Redwings 63	25	at feeder: 26 chickadees 2 titmice 5 cardinals 1 doves 17
27	28 7 Goldfinches	29 mixed pond ducks 71	30	31 Crocuses blooming!	Planted SnapPeas 1	at feeder: 1 chickadees 3 titmice 7 cardinals 2 doves 29

1 Migrant arrival dates

Generic OK

Other stuff happening

3 Abundance numbers for one species

2 First-song dates

4 Feeder visits

A different weather channel

Birds respond to the same changes of season and weather that we do, and they often respond in ways that we can easily notice. For hundreds of years, farmers and others have watched birds and used their observations to help them decide when to plant crops, or when bad weather is on its way. For example, when the Common Loon calls sadly again and again at midday, observers believe that rain is coming soon.

People who feed birds find that birds' daily activities are fairly routine: Northern Cardinals feed at dawn and dusk, Blue Jays arrive at noon, and so on. But bird-watchers also report that these routines will change in the face of a storm or a major change in the weather. Watch for birds feeding busily before predicted heavy snows. Perhaps the birds sense the low pressure, just as a barometer does, and hurry to eat while they can.

Birds that people-watch

We notice what birds do, but do birds notice humans? Probably more than you might think! Bird feeders attract birds: That's one proof that birds notice us. Since people began hunting, many scavenging birds have noticed and benefited from their activities. Even now, Golden Eagles may depend on the remains of deer killed by humans in places like Scotland.

In Africa and Australia, birds called honey-guides connect with people by leading them to bee trees full of honey. After the human

Home bodies
Beginning birders don't have to go far to find any of the three bird species below. These birds are comfortable living close to houses and farms and make themselves useful by feeding on insects that bother both people and livestock.

House Finch adult and fledglings

harvests the honey, the birds help themselves to the remains. It's important to note, though, that birds seem to notice anything that might lead to food, even the activities of other animals.

Some birds seem very comfortable around humans. Perhaps they think human buildings, roadways, neighborhoods, gardens, and farms are their natural habitat. Some probably like the things humans provide, like scraps around the local fast food restaurant and string in our vegetable gardens. So even if we don't *try* to attract some birds, they show up anyway.

Sticks to More than Your Ribs

Cliff Swallows are rare birds who build nests from balls of mud attached under the eaves of buildings. Mud of the right quality isn't always easy to find, but it's vital to successful nesting. One Cliff Swallow pair's nest, discovered by students on an elementary school building in Princeton, Massachusetts, took advantage of humans in a new way. The crafty swallows used baked beans from the cafeteria leftovers bin, managing to build almost an entire nest from this ready supply of good building material!

There are a number of bird species that are found living *only* around humans. House Finches sometimes build their nests in people's wreaths or in their potted plants. Brown-headed Cowbirds hang around cattle, eating insects the cows stir up. Phoebes like to build their moss-decorated mud nests under overhangs, porch roofs, sheds, and cupolas.

Even in the depths of the largest cities, Rock Doves, House Sparrows, and European Starlings thrive. And scientists, trying to increase the population of the endangered Peregrine Falcon, discovered that these birds can live in cities as well. The falcons find Rock Doves delicious!

Eastern Phoebe

Brown-headed Cowbird

Two Who Made a Difference

You're just one person. Can anything you do really make a difference? Yes!
Read these two stories for inspiration.

Silence isn't golden

Less than 50 years ago, chemicals called pesticides were being used with very little control or safety. A biologist, Rachel Carson, noticed that these pesticides were affecting living things. She worried that humans could also be in danger. After studying the matter carefully, she wrote a book called *Silent Spring*. People all over the world read the book and began a huge outcry for change. The chapter that made people most upset was called "And No Birds Sing." People were appalled to think that birds could die by the thousands from something as simple as a lawn spray.

Hats to die for

Hats were popular in the late 1800s, and the bigger the better. Hatters made enormous hats from feathers and even whole birds, killing thousands of beautiful songbirds, herons, and egrets just for their plumes. In 1896, Harriet Hemenway led a small group of women in Boston, Massachusetts, to protest this cruel fashion. They refused to wear feathered hats and convinced their friends, and their friends' friends, to do the same. The movement grew to become the Massachusetts Audubon Society. By 1899, just three years later, 16 other states had Audubon societies of their own.

Act locally *and* globally

If you keep a bird calendar and share your observations with your local bird club, you'll be part of the local bird census (see chapter 4). The census, or count, helps identify areas where birds gather, where they are diverse and abundant. This information can help encourage your city, town, or neighborhood to set aside safe places for birds.

Want to help out in other ways? Think about how you and your family live. Many of the things we do and buy can threaten birds and their habitats. You can make lifestyle decisions that will help birds nearby *and* farther away. Ask your friends and family to help with this. Here's a quick list.

- Buy local and organic foods and snacks.
- Buy only shade-grown coffee (see Made in the Shade, right).
- Don't use pesticides or lawn-care chemicals.
- Turn your lawn into a meadow by mowing only paths, not the whole yard.
- Walk, bike, or take public transportation (don't drive!) to school and to friends' houses.
- Join a local land-trust organization, and find out how you can help save open land near you.

You can also join organizations like The Nature Conservancy, The World Wildlife Fund, your local Audubon Society, and others to find out more ways to help. See Resources for information about other organizations that may interest you.

Running out of Room
Most macaws live year-round in the rapidly disappearing South American rainforest. Half of all macaw species are now classified as endangered.

Made in the Shade

Many migrating birds spend their winters in Central and South America, where tons of coffee is grown on plantations. One way of growing coffee, called the "factory style," pushes local people out, strips the land of its forests and wildlife, spreads pesticides, and eliminates forest bird habitat.

"Fair trade" coffee is organically grown, shade-grown, and bird-safe. Everyone wins when coffee is grown under the shade of the original forest, without harsh chemicals, and by the local people.

We found a baby bird!

People often find baby birds and wonder what to do to help them. Your new knowledge of birds' nests, baby birds, and fledglings can help you decide how to help. First things first:

Where are you?

You're most likely to find baby birds on the ground, often in yards, in open areas like parks, or on roadways. These are areas where birds are easy to see, and where baby birds are likely to get hurt.

Nature knows best . . . usually

It is perfectly "natural" for baby birds to fall from their nests and be separated from their parents. Accidents happen. Often, nothing can help them. The best thing you can do is to help the bird into a safe, natural environment, away from human dangers like cars and cats. Any baby bird found in a natural setting like an open field or forest, where human-related dangers are few, is best left alone. Only bird rehabilitators who specialize in orphan birds can successfully raise and train young birds, and they often fail. Don't try to take it home!

How to help

So you've found a baby bird, let's say in the middle of your lawn. Take a close look to evaluate its condition. Is it:

A nestling altricial baby? Such a baby would be naked, or sparsely feathered, and very young. Often these birds are lying down, their eyes are closed, or they can't move or hop.

Altricial
Barn Swallow
chicks

Is a nest visible and safely reached? If yes, return the baby to its nest. If no, place the baby in a one-pint strawberry basket as an artificial nest, with hay or grass to support it. Tie this nest securely as high as possible in the closest shrub or low tree. Try to ensure it can't be seen or reached by cats or dogs. Leave it alone, and hope the parent birds will find it and care for it. You may not see them, so don't worry. You've done what you can.

A fledgling altricial baby? A bird this age would be nearly the same size as its parents, but a little plumper, with shorter wing and tail feathers. It is trying its wings, but it may not be able to hop or fly to safety. Gently lift the baby and place it in the nearest shrub or tree branch and leave the area. Fledglings may not be visited by their parents very often, and may make very pathetic-sounding cries, but their parents will usually come back.

Obviously injured? Perhaps you can see blood, a wing that hangs funny, or another injury. Get help. Call a wildlife rehabilitator through the local animal shelter, veterinarian, fish and wildlife office, or Audubon Society sanctuaries and facilities.

A precocial baby bird? These birds can walk but still may find themselves in dangerous situations. Ducklings, goslings, killdeer chicks, and others may get into backyards and become trapped by fences. Gently aim the mother with babies in the direction of shelter and safety, and keep commotion, dogs, and cats away. Find some help, if you can. Adults, even policemen, may be necessary when roadways are involved. Your knowledge of local habitats can make a big difference. If, for example, a mother duck is leading ducklings to a pond and is confused by fences or walls, you can help by showing them the way to water. Even with only a little bit of knowledge of birds, you can make a difference. (See p. 35)

Look Before You Leap
This just-hatched Herring Gull chick may look like it's in trouble, but the small depression and the intact egg and feathers beside it tell you it's actually in its own nest.

Precocial Canada Goose gosling

Build a Four-Season Bird Arbor

You can make an arbor from natural materials to invite birds to your backyard, or you can add one to a feeder area. Choose a spot for the arbor that is near your house and visible from a window so you can observe and record all the activities of birds. Note: An adult should help with this project.

You'll need:

- Four flexible tree saplings, each about 12' tall, and no more than 1½" in diameter
- Crowbar
- String, florist's wire, or young outer branches, for binding
- Wool, fibers, seeds, berries, suet, etc. for attracting nesting and feeding birds

1. Cut your saplings. Choose flexible woods like hickory, ash, willow, or oak. Leave the side branches on. If you don't have saplings in your yard, ask your local roads department if they can give you some.

3. Use a crowbar to "punch" four 1-foot-deep holes in the ground, in a rectangular pattern as shown. Insert the base of your four saplings in the holes.

2. Curve the upper half of each sapling by firmly bending the tree into an arch. Begin at the upper end and bend every foot or so of the tree over your knee or a stump.

4. Bring together the tops of two saplings from opposite corners (diagonally) to create an arch. Bind them together with string, their own branches, or coated florists' wire. Hickory bark strips also make tough, natural binding. Repeat this step with the other two saplings.

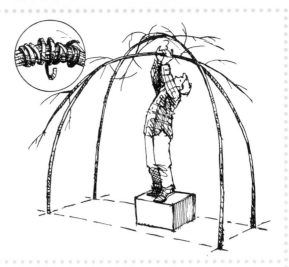

5. Once you have two similar-size arches, connect them at the top center or install a series of short horizontal pieces, ladder style, going up and over. Use wire, twine, bark, or whatever you have available to bind the pieces together. Natural arbors are unlikely to last more than five years, so binding methods needn't be too permanent.

Now you have an arbor! Birds will quickly begin to use it as a perch and a lookout as they scan the area for food. In spring or summer, you can plant beans, sweet peas, or other climbing plants beneath the arbor to grow up its poles and attract insects and birds. In fall and winter, tie seeds and berries to the arbor, or hang feeders and suet on it. In spring, hang bits of string, wool, or fibers to help nesting birds, and tack up orange halves for fruit-eating migrants like Baltimore Orioles.

Build a Nesting Platform

Some birds prefer to nest under overhanging ledges and downed trees. Many will use ledges people have built, if they're made and placed carefully. Barn Swallows, Eastern Phoebes, and House Finches can all be encouraged to nest when a small platform is provided under the overhang of a roof or shed. And, if they're already nesting in the wrong place, such as over your door, you can choose a safer spot for them!

You'll need:

- Two boards, each 8 x 10 x 2"
- Three 2"-long flat-headed nails
- Three 3"-long wood screws
- A flat surface under an overhang, such as the wall of a shed or garage or a protected wall of your house
- An adult to help you if you're not an experienced woodworker

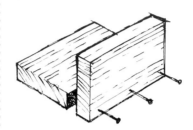

1. Lay the two boards together at right angles along their longest side. Nail the top (platform) piece to the bottom (brace) piece in two or three places.

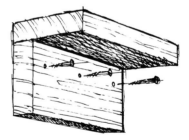

2. Use the screws to attach the platform to your chosen spot. Leave at least 6" of (adult) head room under the overhang.

3. Watch for nesting American Robins, swallows, phoebes or other birds to arrive!

Build a Chickadee Nest Box

Black-capped Chickadees prefer to nest in dead trees at the edges of wooded areas, but they will use nest boxes when their natural nesting sites are scarce. As forested areas grow smaller, large, dead trees become scarce. Nest boxes improve habitat and make a bird's life easier.

The design shown here opens two ways: from the top, so you can see inside without disturbing the nest, and from the side, so you can clean the box easily at the end of the nesting season.

To prepare, sand outside wood surfaces. Drill a centered 1⅛" hole, with its upper edge 1" below the top of the front panel. Cut a 14-degree angle slot into the back of the box near the top, for the insertion of the angle-cut roof.

Note: This project is more challenging than the previous ones and is suitable for people with experience in woodworking and cutting.

Materials

- ⅞ x 10 x 50" rough-cut cedar or pine
- Sixteen 6d (2") long galvanized ring-shank siding nails
- Three 4d (1") galvanized finishing nails, or wood screws to attach dowel (optional)
- Two galvanized #6 x 1½" pan-head screws and washers
- Eyelet screw (optional)
- If using planed lumber, 2" x 4" piece of ¼" galvanized wire mesh hardware cloth. Attach to inside of front, and turn down sharp edges, to aid fledging. Or, rout or score inside front to provide a grip.
- Heavy-duty staples or ¾" 18-gauge wire brads to attach hardware cloth

Tools

- Table saw, saber saw, jigsaw (bevel cuts are required), or carpenter's handsaw and miter box
- Power or hand drill
- 1½" diameter keyhole saw or expansion bit
- ³⁄₁₆" and ¼" drill bits
- Standard or Phillips-head screwdriver, or power drill fitted with screwdriver bits
- Claw hammer
- Tape measure or yard (meter) stick
- Carpenter's square
- Pencil
- Staple gun, sandpaper, light-colored exterior latex house paint, paintbrush (optional)

(continued on next page)

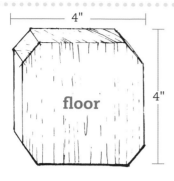

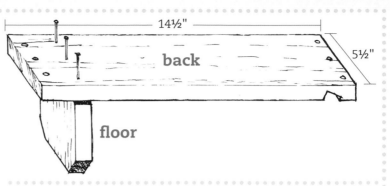

1. Cut ⅝" off each corner of the floor to create drainage holes. Nail the **floor** to the **back**, recessing it ¼" from the bottom to create a drip edge.

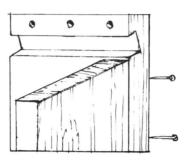

2. Screw or nail **side 1** to the joined **back** and **floor**, leaving a ¼" wide gap at the top for ventilation.

3. Screw or nail the **front** to the joined **floor** and **side**, again being sure to leave a ¼" recess at the bottom.

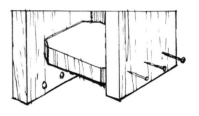

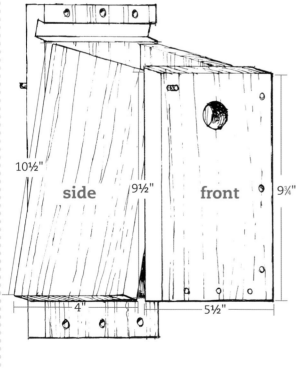

4. Attach **side 2** (the clean-out door) only at the top, using two 4d galvanized finishing nails to create a pivot. *Important:* The pivot nails must be exactly opposite each other for proper opening. Using predrilled holes will help you properly locate these. Be sure to leave the necessary ventilation gap on this side as well. Add a centered galvanized #6 x 1½" pan-head screw and washer near the bottom of this side to line up with the recessed floor. This will secure the side in place. Alternatively, use a right-angle screw.

5. Fit the **roof** into the angled slot cut in the **back** and hold it there by placing a single centered #6 pan-head screw and washer through the top into the top edge of the front. You can also use an eyelet screw and washer; this eliminates the need for a screwdriver each time you open the box.

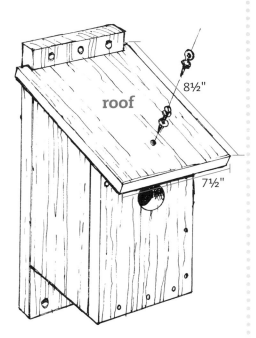

Mounting the box

The nest box should be between 4½ and 10 feet above the ground. Be sure to attach a sheet metal cone, stovepipe, PVC plastic, or other baffle to the support pipe, post, or tree, to keep predators from entering the box. Place a 1" layer of wood chips or shavings into the box.

Finding a site

Place your chickadee box near the edge of a forest or a stand of trees, or in a forest clearing. Choose a spot that gets sun for 40 to 60 percent of the day.

Nest Box Maintenance

Check nest boxes once a week, as they sometimes become targets for predators. Looking in usually won't bother the birds, and you'll be able to see how many eggs have been laid and whether predators or parasites are a problem.

6

Incredible Birds

You never forget your first glimpse of a glorious peacock. A swirling flock of starlings can make you dizzy with awe. Birds are amazing in all kinds of ways, and the longer you study them, the more fascinating they become. Each species has its special abilities, its particular ways of doing things, its remarkable features.

In the pages that follow, you'll meet a whole gallery of notable birds. Most of them are North American, so you might have a chance to admire their exploits yourself at some point in your bird-watching adventures. Welcome to the Avian Hall of Fame!

The Original "Big Bird"

Using fossil bones, scientists have estimated that the heaviest birds that ever lived were the Elephant Birds of Madagascar. Flightless birds, with eagle-like, can-opener beaks, they weighed close to *one thousand pounds*. An Elephant Bird egg weighed more than 18 pounds, about as much as 10 dozen chicken eggs, and held roughly two gallons of fluid. New Zealand's similar extinct birds, Moas, were 13 feet tall. Both of these giants were alive just a few thousand years ago.

King of Blue
Found in the southern and southwestern United States, the Blue Grosbeak is a startlingly beautiful, colorful bird that prefers weedy areas.

Fastest runner

Roadrunners and **Wild Turkeys** are probably the fastest birds in North America. At 25 and 20 miles per hour, respectively, they're just able to outrun humans, who can do about 18 miles per hour. Mee-meep!

Tallest and heaviest

North America's tallest bird is the Whooping Crane, taller than the average 10-year-old child, at 5 feet. But Whooping Cranes aren't as heavy as **Trumpeter Swans,** who have the water to help hold them up. They weigh in at 38 pounds, a fact they can bugle about as the heaviest birds in North America.

Fastest flier

Flying straight ahead. **Swifts** are probably the fastest fliers, easily reaching more than 150 miles per hour. Try that in a car and the only thing you'd win is a big, fat speeding ticket! Note that all the fastest-flying birds have long, thin, pointy wings, especially compared to soaring birds.

Diving through the air. Gravity can help a diving Peregrine Falcon speed downward toward its prey at almost 200 miles per hour. That's about as fast as the high-speed Japanese bullet train. *After* lunch, the same bird may flap along at "only" 50 miles per hour.

Smallest

Trying to spot the **Calliope Hummingbird** can be a challenge. It's just three inches long from tip to tail and weighs about half as much as a teabag. Have your binoculars handy!

Widest wingspan

Trumpeter Swans can carry their bulk on 8-foot wings, but North America's **California Condor,** along with the slightly larger Andean Condor from South America, have wingspans of around 10 feet. They can lift their body weights of 20 to 25 pounds (can you lift *your* body weight?). And if you've heard that albatrosses have the widest wingspans, you're right. The Wandering Albatross's wingspan can exceed 11 feet! But only two species of albatross ever get close enough to the California coast to observe, and they have 7-foot wingspans.

Most miles flown

Almost all birds are "superbirds" when it comes to distance flight. Even the tiny hummingbird flies hundreds of miles in migration, not pausing for food or rest. The **Bobolink** flies the farthest of our inland birds: Its wintering grounds in southern South America lie over 2,000 miles from the great meadows of the central United States. And the Arctic Tern flies 11,000 miles one way, then returns the same distance on its journeys between the Arctic and the Antarctic.

Highest fliers

If the Alps and Himalayas sat right in the middle of your migration path, what would you do? Increase your altitude, or find a way around them? Geese seem to set the high-flying standard: The **Bar-headed Goose** flies as high as 30,000 feet to clear the mountains (that's taller than 20 Empire State Buildings put together). The question is: Do they ever look down?

Deepest divers

Common Loons probably take gold medals in diving for both depth and time spent underwater. They can dive down more than 100 feet and spend several minutes there, dining on fish and coming up not far from where they started.

Most talkative

Magpie flocks keep up a steady stream of cackles, whistles, and imitations. Northern Mockingbirds make themselves popular by singing at night and driving people nearby crazy.

Oldest

The oldest birds in the world are generally the largest. Cranes, for example, live up to 60 years, but ravens, eagles, gulls, and geese can also live, at least in captivity, for more than 50 years. **Great Horned Owls** have been known to live to the age of 100. In the wild, where danger is common and food can be scarce, most small birds live only a few years. Larger birds like ravens, ducks, geese, and raptors live longer, closer to 20 or 30 years.

How do we know? Most records of bird life in the wild come from banding programs, in which birds are captured wearing bands with dates on them. Several species of ducks have been shown, through banding, to reach 15 to 20 years old in the wild.

Most creative with food

And their parents *like* this! In this category, we have a three-way tie. Phalarope use their flexible feet to spin in shallow water like a child's toy top. They then poke with their beaks, grabbing plankton, shrimps, and insect larvae stirred up from the bottom. Northern Shrikes are songbirds that look like little hawks. They're pretty good at catching and tearing insects, small mammals, and other prey. They then pin what they've caught on a plant's thorns or in the Y-shaped crotches of shrubs. Shrikes often store many food items in one tree or shrub and return to it later to feed. And the **Herring Gull** drops clams from 50 feet up onto hard surfaces like roads and rocks to break the shells open.

Best dancer

Whooping Cranes win this one, and it's no wonder they need an outdoor dance floor! They bow to each other, then leap 3 feet into the air, spreading their glorious 7-foot wings, arching their heads over their backs, and continuing to jump like pogo sticks. A few species of birds, including the male American Woodcock and Horned Lark, dance in midair, taking dizzying flights spiraling up from 200 to 800 feet, then zooming back to earth at almost the same point of takeoff.

Best mimic

Everyone knows at least one parrot who can imitate the human voice. But we've got a lot of mimics out there in the wild world as well. The mockingbird family, including the **Gray Catbird,** Northern Mockingbird, and Brown Thrasher, are the hands-down champions, easily able to copy dozens of other birds' songs. They mimic both songs and alarm call notes. Mockingbirds have even learned to imitate car alarms and other routine human noises near their habitats.

Loves to pick a fight

Jays are pretty fierce in defense of their fledglings, but the champions here must be **Kingbirds,** members of a group scientists call the "tyrant flycatchers" because of their tempers. They attack and try to chase other birds away from their territories without fear. They'll take on anything that moves, no matter how big, including hawks, eagles, coyotes, and people.

Least likely to succeed

The **Bald Eagle** may be our national bird, but it's a scavenger, especially near water, snatching dead fish, feeding on ice-downed deer carcasses, and the like. There's nothing wrong with taking what life hands you, right? Well, what about stealing? Bald Eagles will rob just-caught fish from hard-working Ospreys, and gulls will wait around for diving ducks to surface with their food, then grab it and fly. It's a jungle out there!

Handiest with a tool

Brown-headed Nuthatches don't bother with needle-nosed pliers. They use pinecone scales to poke and pry out insects from crevices in tree bark.

Best synchronized flying

Sandpipers take the gold, creating whirling clouds like a school of fish as they fly just a few inches apart in apparent synchrony. They probably do this to look bigger and startle their enemies, but it's also the sign of a remarkable brain.

Best dressed

This one depends on the judges. The Scissor-tailed Flycatcher will certainly catch your attention, if you live in its small range around Texas and Oklahoma. Its tail is longer than the bird itself! The **Painted Bunting** *(above, right)* is a colorful songbird, with patches of three shockingly bright colors: a scarlet breast and belly, blue head and neck, and parakeet-green back and tail. Some judges prefer the Vermilion Flycatcher, the reddest bird you'll ever see, with a contrasting black mask. And, of course, hummingbirds of many species, with their special iridescent feathers, reflect rainbows of color. Even the **Ring-necked Pheasant** has its fans, but the male Purple Gallinule may startle you the most: Look out for its bright yellow legs, grape-purple body with green overtones, red and yellow bill, and baby-blue spot above the bill.

Biggest bullies

"We were just protecting ourselves!" "But I don't even eat Red-winged Blackbirds!" That's how the testimony might go in a case where a flock of Red-winged Blackbirds is accused of mobbing a Red-tailed Hawk. Small birds (such as **crows**) will often join forces to drive hawks, **owls,** ravens, and other large birds from their areas, even on occasion killing the larger birds. They may mob both perched birds and birds in flight. If nothing else, it can be a great way for bird-watchers to find raptors!

Most time spent preening

Everybody gets a prize in this category. Birds spend a lot of time cleaning themselves. It helps remove insects and keep the feathers waterproof. Oh, and it also means they look their best in photographs like these!

Most dramatic

Some birds that nest on the ground have developed great acting ability to protect their nests. The **Killdeer** pretends to be injured when a predator comes near. This charade is meant to lure the predator after the adult bird, far away from nest and eggs. But what happens if a deer decides to come too close to the eggs? It won't work to look wounded, because deer aren't predators. Now it's time to act tough: Go right in the face of that deer and scare it away!

Ready, Set, "Flun"!

Birds move underwater by pushing against the water with their wings and propelling with their feet, so diving is a little like running and flying at the same time. Most ducks swim and dive using their feet. The auk family, which includes birds like the Dovekie and the Black Guillemot, is especially equipped for underwater "flying," so they can fly both in air and water. That puts them ahead of **penguins**: Those champion wing divers are flightless on land.

Appendix

Glossary

Abundance. The number of individual birds within a species

Adapt. Change over many years

Alarm note. Short, urgent call

Altricial. Term for young birds that are born naked and unable to walk, with eyes closed, and that stay in the nest for two or three weeks after birth

Alula. Small group of stiff feathers that jut from the top of the wing, move independently from flight feathers, and control flow of air over the wing

Barb. Tiny branch that grows from the shaft of a feather; many barbs form the vane

Barbule. Tiny hook on the branch of a barb that interlocks with others to form a "web" that creates the feather vane

Belly. Underpart of a bird's body between mid-trunk and base of tail, where legs join the body

Bill. Bony outgrowth of a bird's skull; also called a beak

Biodiversity. The dazzling variety of life on earth

Breast. Underpart of a bird's body between mid-trunk and neck area

Bristles. Hairlike feathers found mostly around the eyes, nostrils, and mouths of birds; give birds the sense of touch

Call. Usually simple and nonmusical, a vocalization indicating a bird's location and "mood"

Carpo-metacarpus. Second digit and combined wrist–hand bone of bird

Cavity nester. Bird that uses tree holes and human-made boxes for nesting

Census. A record of birds that observers see or hear during a specified time period; usually performed twice a year, in June and December, to measure abundance and diversity

Chip call. Short, loud, one-syllable vocalization

Clutch. The number of eggs laid and incubated during one nesting period

Contour feathers. Feathers that form the basic outer shape of the bird, including wings, tail, and body

Crepuscular. Active at dawn and dusk

Crest. Elongated feathers on the top of some birds' heads

Crown. The top part of a bird's head, generally above and behind the eye

Density. Number of birds of the same species that live in a certain area

Diversity. The number of bird species in an area

Diurnal. Active in daylight

Down feathers. Soft feathers that insulate birds against extreme temperatures

Endangered. Having very low or rapidly declining population

Exhalation. Breathing out

Extinct. Having died out

Eye ring. Contrasting colored area around the entire eye

Eyeline. Contrasting thin line extending from the corners of a bird's eyes, parallel to the beak

Feathers. Body outgrowths, originally scales, that have evolved over time to keep birds warm and dry, and to help with flight

Fecal sac. Plasticlike pouch, clear or white with a dark end, containing a baby songbird's body waste

Flank. Underpart of a bird's body, on each side above the belly and under the wings

Fledgling. Baby bird that has left the nest but may still be dependent on parents

Flyways. Much-traveled migration routes across continents

Grassland birds. Species that require fields, meadows, and other grassy places to survive

Habitat. Natural environment

Humerus. Upper bone of wing

Incubation. Period during which parent birds transfer warmth and moisture from their bodies to their eggs by sitting on them

Keratin. Protein that forms human nails, and birds' claws, feathers, and scales

Mandibles. The upper and lower halves of a bill

Mantle. Feathers of the back and folded wings, especially on gulls

Migrate. Move from place to place according to the seasons

Nestling. Baby bird while still in the nest

Niche. Birds' occupation, largely related to food needs

Nocturnal. Active at night

Pigment. Natural coloring of animal tissue

Precocial. Term for young birds that hatch with their eyes open, able to run or swim; they leave the nest within a day or two of hatching

Primaries. Large flight feathers that form part of the wing surface (see also secondaries)

Rump. Upper part of a bird's body, above the base of the tail

Scales. Outgrowths that cover most birds' feet and toes; can be temporary

Scavenger. Animal that feeds on other dead animals

Secondaries. Bird's long flight feathers, closer to the body than the primaries

Semiplumes. Feathers that fill the space between contour feathers and the next layer of feathers; have large shafts with downy barbs

Shaft. Hollow, round stem of a feather to which barbs are attached to form the vane

Shrub layer. Forest vegetation that reaches from the ground to about ten feet above the ground

Slot. Space between primary feathers on the wing tips that reduces pressure above the wing and gives lift, and directs air flowing over and under the wings

Song. Short or long series of notes that often sound musical; usually heard in spring or summer to define territory

Speculum. Iridescent secondary feathers which, when folded, create a colorful patch that can only be seen from a certain angle; often seen in ducks

Superciliary. Line above each eye of some birds

Syrinx. Unique structure in bird's windpipe, halfway to the stomach, which can stretch or enlarge to create and control sound

Tail. On birds, small outgrowth made up of sturdy feathers and a tiny bit of bone or flesh

Talon. Hooked claw

Territory. Place that birds claim as theirs; displays of feathers, color, call notes, and songs help define a bird's territory

Ulna. The forearm bone

Undertail. Feathers that cover the base of the tail, under the bird

Vane. Flat portion of a feather, made up of hundreds of tiny parallel branches

Vertebrates. Animals with backbones

Webbing. Thin, flexible skin that joins the bones of some birds' feet; allows them to swim on the water's surface and below it

Wingbar. Contrasting white or light lines on the upper part of the folded wing of some birds, created by white tips of covert wing feathers

Resources for Expanding Your Enjoyment of Birds

There are plenty of bird books and other resources available out there depending upon your interests. Whether you're interested in more advanced identification, new habitat exploration, bird migration, or some other aspect of bird life, the following list can help you expand your horizons.

Books and more

First Guides

National Audubon First Guides: Birds
Scholastic, 1998.
Here are 50 common species with other great information. A good portable first guide.

Smithsonian Kids' Field Guides
 Birds of North America East
 Birds of North America West
New York: Dorling Kindersley, 2001.
Probably the best first guide, with over a hundred species for each region. Exciting and informative format and layout, and lots of trivia as well as identification information.

Golden Guides: Birds
Saint Martin's Press, 2001.
Lots of people grew up with these guides, and they are still loved for their simple, clear illustrations and reliable information.

Field Guides

Peterson Field Guides
 Birds: Eastern
 Birds: Western
Houghton Mifflin, 2002.
We still like these, after 50 years. Roger Tory Peterson invented the idea of field guides for everyday people. Illustrations help you see all the field marks on one bird; range maps, notes on calls and songs make this one of the better field guides even now.

The Sibley Field Guides
 Birds of Eastern North America
 Birds of Western North America
Alfred A. Knopf, 2003.
Not really field guides because they have so much information, and they're pretty big! Immature birds, great tips for ID, and beautiful illustrations make these books your best bet as a table resource for lots of bird questions.

Smithsonian Handbooks: Birds of . . .
by Fred Alsop. DK Publishing Inc.
These handbooks (there are many!) have been developed for New England, Texas, the Mid-Atlantic, Western Region, and other areas. They're packed with great information and high-quality illustrations.

Digging Deeper

Birds' Nests and Eggs, by Mel Boring and Linda Garrow. Sagebrush Education Resources, 1996. Everything you need to know about nests, with activities and observation galore.

Secrets of the Nest, by Joan Dunning. Houghton Mifflin Co., 1994.
Beautifully illustrated and thoughtful.

Bird Tracks and Signs, by Mark Elbroch, Eleanor Marks, C. Diane Boretos. Stackpole Books, 2001.
An adult resource organized by common species and full of pictures of feathers, tracks, scats, and other interesting tidbits. Worth it just to ID all those feathers you'll find!

The Sibley Guide to Bird Life and Behavior, by David Allen Sibley. Alfred A. Knopf, 2001.
Lots of text, so it looks difficult, but use the index to find the information you're seeking.

Flight of the Golden Plover, by Debbie S. Miller and Daniel Van Zyle. Alaska Northwest Books, 1996.

For you western birders, a long-distance journey from Hawaii to Alaska.

The Bird Almanac, by David Bird. Firefly Books, 2004.
Calls itself "A Guide to Essential Facts and Figures of the World's Birds." Fun to browse if it's bird facts you're after.

Helping Orphaned or Injured Wild Birds. Storey Publishing, 1999.

For Younger Readers

Crinkleroot's Guide to Knowing the Birds, by Jim Arnosky. Simon and Schuster, 1992.

About Birds: A Guide for Children, by Cathryn and John Sill. Peachtree, 1997.

Eyewitness: Bird, by David Burnie. Dorling-Kindersley, 2000.

The Burgess Bird Book for Children, by Thornton Burgess. Dover, 2003.

CDs and Cassettes

Birding by Ear: Eastern
Birding by Ear: Western
Walton, Sill, et al.
Boston: Houghton-Mifflin Co., 1999 and 2002.
Don't forget song as an ID tool and to increase your understanding of bird language and behavior. This is really the only bird song cassette or CD you'll need at first. It groups birds by the type of songs they make (trills, sing-songs, etc.) and covers only the most common birds.

Videos, DVDs (fiction and non–fiction)

Fly Away Home (DVD, 2004)

Winged Migration, Jacques Perrin (DVD, 2003)

The Life of Birds, David Attenborough, BBC Video (DVD, 2002)

Web sites

americanbirding.org
Workshops, tours, festivals, and other bird-related activities; a portion of the site is designed for young birders.

audubon.org
National Audubon's Web site is full of bird news, ways you can help, information, and interesting tidbits. They also publish a monthly magazine.

audubon.org/bird/cat/
In case you can't find it on the main site, here's the address for cat and bird advice from National Audubon: great tips for protecting birds.

mbr-pwrc.usgs.gov/
The U.S. Department of the Interior and the U.S. Geological Survey run the Patuxent Wildlife Research Center in Maryland. Its Web site has a wealth of information about birds, including beautiful photographs, recorded songs, and annual census results.

cws-scf.ec.gc.ca/index_e.cfm
The Canadian Wildlife Service Web site is a source of information on Canada's breeding bird survey, bird trends, conservation, and more.

Associations

National Audubon Society
700 Broadway
New York, NY 10003
The Society's Web site (see above) can help you find the state Audubon Society nearest to your home.

American Birding Association
P.O. Box 6599
Colorado Springs, Colorado 80934
This association aims to inspire people to enjoy and protect birds. (See Web site above.)

Index

Other Storey Titles You Might Enjoy

Raptor! by Christyna M. and René Laubach and Charles W.G. Smith
Named a 2002 Outstanding Science Trade Book by the Children's Book Council/National Science Teachers Association. Packed with photos and detailed information about eagles, hawks, osprey, vultures, and other raptors. 128 pages; paperback. ISBN: 1-58017-445-0.

Weather! by Rebecca Rupp
Named a 2005 Teachers' Choice Award for Children's Books winner. Facts, statistics, and explanations that kids find irresistible for understanding wind, rain, tornadoes, snow, lightning, and more. Includes 22 science experiments. 144 pages; paperback. ISBN: 1-58017-420-5.

The Kids' Building Workshop by Craig and Barbara Robertson
These projects bring parents and children together to build 15 fun and useful items. Lively photographs, illustrations, and explanatory text teach kids essential skills. 144 pages; paperback. ISBN: 1-58017-488-4.

Recycled Crafts Box by Laura C. Martin
Kids can make 40 great crafts projects with colorful easy-to-follow instructions. Plastic picnic plates become a bouquet of flowers; yogurt containers are fashioned into little dolls. 96 pages; paperback. ISBN: 1-58017-522-8.

WoodsWalk by Henry W. Art and Michael W. Robbins
Winner of the *Learning © Magazine* Teachers' Choice℠ Award For the Family. A kids' guide to observing the wonders of the woods, using all five senses, throughout the seasons and in all regions of North America. Full-color photos. 128 pages; paperback. ISBN: 1-58017-452-3.

Horse Games & Puzzles for Kids by Cindy A. Littlefield
More than 100 puzzles, activities, riddles, quizzes, and games to keep young horse-lovers happy and busy for hours. 144 pages; paperback. ISBN: 1-58017-538-4.

Bird-watching Quiz

Look at this picture carefully for 30 seconds. Then turn the page.

Bird-watching Quiz

Examine the picture on the previous page. Then, without looking back, answer the questions below. Give yourself two minutes to take the quiz.

1. What color is the bird with a crest (a tuft standing up on its head)?

_____

2. Is the upside-down bird the smallest or largest in the picture?

_____

3. What color is the largest bird?

_____

4. What is the red-breasted bird doing?

_____

5. What colors are the birds that are interacting?

_____

6. Does the largest or smallest bird have the longest bill?

_____

7. Does the smallest or largest bird have the least obvious tail?

_____

8. What's the fattest bird doing?

_____

Now check your answers. If you answered questions 1, 3, 4, and 5 quickly and easily, you have a good memory for color. If you were quick to answer questions 1, 6, 7, and 8, you're great at seeing shapes. If answers came easily to you for questions 2, 3, 6, and 7, you have a knack for observing size. And finally, if you had no trouble with questions 2, 4, 5, and 8, you tend to notice behavior most easily.

We included this quiz to show you that every person sees things differently and notices different aspects of what he or she sees. Some people can see a bird and tell you just what size it was; others can't say if it was the size of a mailbox or an apple, but they know it was blue and red.